Human Resources
as the Wealth of Nations

ECONOMIC DEVELOPMENT SERIES

General Editor
Gerald M. Meier, Professor of International Economics, Stanford University

Published
FINANCIAL DEEPENING IN ECONOMIC DEVELOPMENT
   Edward S. Shaw
ECONOMIC THEORY AND THE UNDERDEVELOPED COUNTRIES
   H. Myint

Human Resources
as the Wealth of Nations

Frederick H. Harbison

New York
OXFORD UNIVERSITY PRESS
London   1973   Toronto

A Project of

THE INTER-UNIVERSITY STUDY OF
HUMAN RESOURCES IN NATIONAL DEVELOPMENT

and

THE INDUSTRIAL RELATIONS SECTION
PRINCETON UNIVERSITY

The Inter-University Study of Human Resources in National Development
was formerly known as
The Inter-University Study of Labor Problems in Economic Development

Introduction to the Economic Development Series

Two centuries ago it all began with *The Wealth of Nations*; today it is called the Poverty of Nations. If economics has always been asked to propose means of social betterment, and if economists are, as Lord Keynes suggested, the trustees of the possibility of civilization—then the problems of world poverty will persistently challenge each generation of economists. But what is new for this generation is the concentrated effort by so many countries to undertake conscious programs of economic development. With the heightened awareness of world inequalities, development policies have been deliberately adopted on a national basis and supported by international institutions.

The time has come for a reappraisal of this experience. This Economic Development Series has therefore been designed to take a hard look at the central problems and strategic policy issues that have emerged to the forefront of development efforts. Recognizing that it has become impossible and undesirable for any one author to attempt to cover the entire subject of economic development, this series concentrates on a set of special problems analyzed by authors who are widely recognized authorities in their respective fields and who have had extensive experience in the developing countries. Each author offers an incisive study of a specific problem area that now requires more understanding by students and practitioners of development alike. The treatment in each volume emphasizes both experience and theory. Taken together, the volumes in this Series formulate a number of policies that may be better designed to cope with some of the most troublesome problems of development.

G. M. MEIER

Preface

For the last fifteen years I have been concerned with manpower as the critical element in the development of modern nations. But in the course of these years my perceptions and ideas have undergone considerable change. Originally, in connection with the Ashby Commission, I was concerned with estimation of high-level manpower requirements for development of Nigeria's modern sector. Later in collaboration with Charles A. Myers (cf. *Education, Manpower and Economic Growth,* McGraw-Hill, 1964), I became interested in analyzing the relationship between economic growth and educational development. Then, four years ago I got entranced with the problems of quantitative measurement of modernization and development (cf. *Quantitative Analyses of Modernization and Development,* Industrial Relations Section, Princeton University, 1971 with Joan Maruhnic and Jane R. Resnick), and very shortly afterward with that amorphous but critically important no-man's land called "nonformal education." Currently, I am wrapped up in problems of sector analysis and comprehensive planning for development and utilization of human resources in modernizing nations.

In this volume I have attempted to present an approach to national development based upon the simple idea that human resources are the ultimate basis of the wealth of nations. From this perspective, the goals of development are the maximum possible utilization of human beings in productive activity and the fullest possible development of the skills, knowledge, and capacities of the labor force. If these goals are pursued, then others such as economic growth, higher levels of living, and more equitable distribution of income are thought to be the likely consequences.

This approach is not new. As indicated in the text, it is in many respects similar to that of Dudley Seers and his colleagues who carried forward the studies of employment generation in Colombia and Ceylon for the ILO. Other economists, who have lately been questioning GNP as the sole measure of progress, may agree in part with my approach, but none, I expect, would accept it completely. This book sets forth only my perspective as a teacher and scholar, and I make no claim to a constituency of followers.

Many persons contributed to this book, for the most part unknowingly. I have been greatly influenced by ideas of many colleagues in the field, principally John Hilliard, Eugene Staley, George Tobias, Robert d'A. Shaw, Guy Hunter, and Irwin Solomon. I am grateful to my partners in the Inter-University Study of Human Resources in National Development (formerly the Inter-University Study of Labor Problems in Economic Development), Clark Kerr, Charles A. Myers, and John Dunlop, for their "enthusiastic skepticism" of the whole project. And, finally, I wish to acknowledge the insights, constructive ideas, and devastating criticism of my graduate students at Princeton.

I am particularly grateful to Joan Maruhnic who, as my research assistant, developed the charts, tables, and quantitative data, made searching analyses of the pertinent literature, insisted on deletion of many passages which, if published, would certainly have tarnished my reputation, and assumed the painstaking tasks of editing the manuscript and reading the printed proofs and pushing the volume through into the production process.

I wish also to acknowledge the financial assistance of the Ford Foundation and the Carnegie Corporation which, through the Inter-University Study, helped to finance this project. And, finally, to Gerald M. Meier for inviting me to prepare this volume for the Oxford University Press Series on Economic Development as well as for his most constructive suggestions for revision on the first draft of the manuscript.

Princeton, N. J.   FREDERICK H. HARBISON
July 4, 1972

Contents

Human Resources
as the Wealth of Nations

1 | Perspectives on Progress

The central thesis of this book is that human resources—not capital, nor income, nor material resources—constitute the ultimate basis for the wealth of nations. Capital and natural resources are passive factors of production; human beings are the active agents who accumulate capital, exploit natural resources, build social, economic, and political organizations, and carry forward national development. Clearly, a country which is unable to develop the skills and knowledge of its people and to utilize them effectively in the national economy will be unable to develop anything else.

Before proceeding further some definitions are necessary: "human resources" are the energies, skills, talent, and knowledge of people which are, or which potentially can or should be, applied to the production of goods or the rendering of useful services. Thus, the term connotes man in relationship to the world of work, and such work involves producing things and providing services of all kinds in the social, political, cultural, and economic development of nations. The "human resources approach" to national development, therefore, is people-oriented, though it does not presume to encompass the full range of human ambitions or endeavors. Man may work to live; hopefully he lives for more than work. Indeed, the energies and skills of people as members of the labor force are but one dimension of human development which embraces as well the thoughts, motives, beliefs, feelings, aspirations, and culture of human beings beyond and outside of work. But in economic terms, the wealth of a nation can be expressed in terms of the level of development and the effectiveness of the utilization of human energies, skills, and knowledge for useful purposes.

The limitation of this perspective to the labor-force-oriented activities of people poses some problems. In advanced countries, the labor force can be defined as including all those who are employed by others or are self-employed as well as those who are unemployed and who are seeking work. But even here there are technical questions of definitions, which become more complicated when one attempts to identify those who are underemployed or sub-employed. In the newly developing countries, the concept of the labor force is much less clear. In some cases, it covers only persons employed for wages or salaries and those seeking work in the modern sectors. This might then include only a fraction, perhaps as little as 5 per cent, of the active population which is presumably related to work on small farms or in subsistence activities in both rural and urban areas. Here the active population is estimated by calculating (where statistics are available) the proportion of the population of "working age" (perhaps those between fourteen and sixty-five years of age) and making assumptions about the proportion of females in this active age group who are thought to be "not working" or to be seeking work.

For practical purposes it is necessary in many of the less developed countries to use the active population as the best available proxy for the labor force. In the newly developing countries, moreover, the concept of open unemployment in the modern-sector enclaves has limited usefulness, and the estimation of "underemployment," "disguised unemployment," and "very low productivity employment" must be based largely on informed guesses rather than actual statistics. It must be recognized, therefore, that human resources (or that part of human activity and effort related to the labor force) cannot be defined or measured with any degree of precision in the less developed countries. The human resources specialist is thus forced to base his analysis on broad orders of magnitude as well as intuitive judgment.

THE MEASUREMENT OF DEVELOPMENT AND MODERNIZATION

According to orthodox economic doctrine, the wealth of nations is measured by income, or more precisely by Gross National Product (GNP) or Gross Domestic Product (GDP) per capita. Thus, a wealthy country is a high income country; advanced nations are by definition those with high GNP per capita; and underdeveloped countries are characterized by very low income per head. Rates of growth, or progress along the road of modernization, are most commonly measured by annual increments in national income or product expressed in monetary terms.

But should income maximization be the supreme or even the primary objective of national economic policy? Are not other goals—for example, minimization of unemployment, maximization of education and knowledge, better health, limitation of population growth, or improvement in the environment—of equal or greater importance? Perhaps in their devout commitment to GNP as the primary measure of progress, economists have developed a "tunnel vision" perspective of the development of nations. But some are now beginning to argue that the GNP approach should be stripped of its sanctity; it is time, they say, to dethrone GNP as the major goal of development policy, at least in the Third World countries.[1]

There are, indeed, a great many ways of measuring development and modernization, and the ranking of countries on the ladder of progress may vary widely depending upon which indicators may be chosen. This can be demonstrated by ranking twenty-five countries according to four statistical indicators: (1) GNP per capita; (2) an index of educational development; (3) an index of nutrition; and (4) an indicator of health. The rankings are shown on Figures 1.1-1.4.

---

1. For further elaboration of this viewpoint, see in particular, International Labour Office, *Towards Full Employment, A Programme for Colombia* (Geneva, 1970). For a short summary, see Dudley Seers, "New Approaches Suggested by the Colombia Employment Program," *International Labour Review* Vol. 102, No. 4 (October 1970), pp. 377-89.

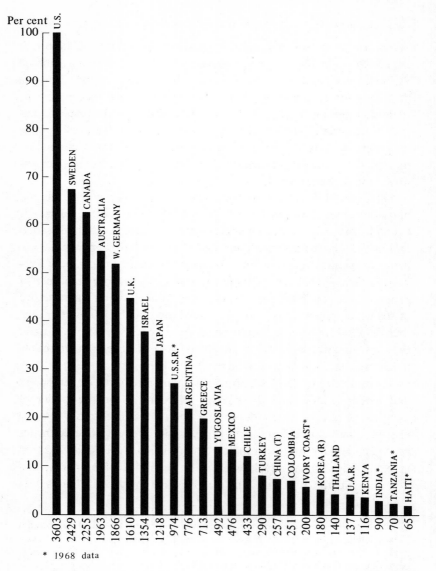

Figure 1.1   GNP per capita—1969
(in 1964 U.S. $ at factor cost)

* 1968 data

SOURCE: IBRD World Tables

6

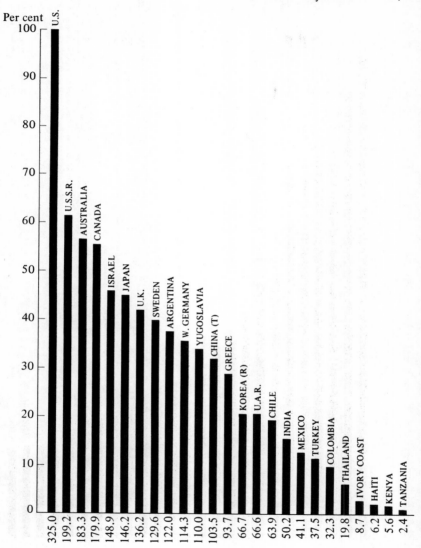

Figure 1.2   Educational enrollment index
(Harbison-Myers index 1965)

SOURCE: Harbison, Maruhnic, and Resnick, *Quantitative Analyses of Moderni-zation and Development,* Appendix VI.

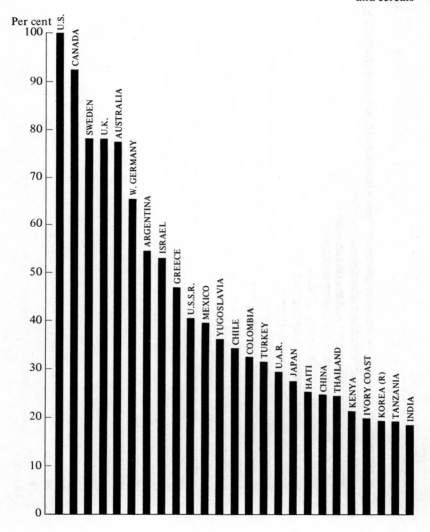

Figure 1.3 Nutrition index
Calories per capita per day divided by per
cent calories per capita per day from starches
and cereals

SOURCE: Harbison, Maruhnic, and Resnick, *Quantitative Analyses of Modernization and Development,* Appendix VIII. A.

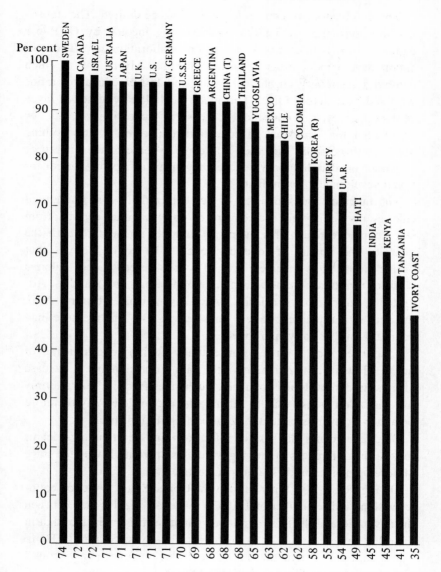

Figure 1.4   Life expectancy (at birth)

SOURCE: Harbison, Maruhnic, and Resnick, *Quantitative Analyses of Modernization and Development,* Appendix VIII. A.

9

These indicators, of course, leave much to be desired. The statistical and conceptual difficulties in measuring income by GNP per capita are widely understood and need no elaboration here. The education development measure is the Harbison-Myers index, which combines secondary enrollment ratios and higher education ratios weighted by a factor of five.[2] This index is admittedly biased in favor of the upper levels of education; it measures "schooling capacity" or flow rather than the stock of education manpower, it says nothing about strategic skills, nor does it attempt to indicate the quality or relevance of schooling provided. Its only virtue as a proxy for educational development is simplicity.

The nutrition index consists of per capita daily consumption of calories divided by the percentage of daily calories derived from starches and cereals. This indicator attempts to measure both the quantity and quality of food consumed. The notion here is that proper nutrition is inversely related to the percentage of calories derived from nonprotein foods made up of cereals and starches. Admittedly, our "adjusted calorie" proxy is somewhat arbitrary. Also, the data in many cases are less than perfect. But this measure may be useful for illustrative purposes.

Life expectancy at birth is conceptually a fairly good indicator of health. However, the reliability of the data is questionable in the case of most underdeveloped countries. Such rates frequently relate only to registration areas (usually urban); the proportions may therefore be under- or over-estimated in nonreporting rural districts.

But, recognizing all these qualifications and shortcomings, let us look at the differences in ranking which result from viewing the stage of development from these four perspectives:

On Figure 1.1 (GNP per capita) the United States is the top country with an index number of 100. On this chart the distance between the advanced and the least developed countries is greater than that in the other three charts. For example, the six lowest countries (Haiti, Tanzania, India, Kenya, the U.A.R., and Thailand) have only about 2 to 4 per cent of the GNP of the United States.

2. See, Frederick H. Harbison and Charles A. Myers, *Education, Manpower and Economic Growth* (New York: McGraw-Hill, 1964), Chap. 3.

On Figure 1.2 (the education index) India and the U.A.R. have, respectively, about 15 and 20 per cent of the score for the top country, which is again the United States. They are now ninth and eleventh from the bottom. Also Japan, Israel, U.S.S.R., China (Taiwan), and Korea (Republic) score much higher on the education index than on the GNP index. The opposite is true for Ivory Coast, West Germany, and Sweden.

Turning to the nutrition index (Figure 1.3), we find that the United States is again the top country. In this case the five lowest countries (India, Tanzania, Korea, Ivory Coast, and Kenya) are at about 20 per cent of the level of the United States. Most of the advanced countries (excepting the United States) and most of the Third World countries do better on this index than on either the GNP or education indices. Clearly, the disparity between the advanced and the least developed countries is narrower; closing the gap would thus be much easier in the case of nutrition.

Figure 1.4 (life expectancy as an index of health) is particularly significant. Here Sweden is in top place, followed very closely by Canada, Israel, Australia, Japan, the United Kingdom, the United States, and West Germany. The lowest five countries (Ivory Coast, Tanzania, Kenya, India, and Haiti) range from about 45 to 65 per cent of Sweden's level. The gap between the advanced and the less developed countries is much narrower even than in the case of the nutrition index.

A number of inferences may be drawn from examination of these crude measures. All of the measures are significantly correlated, but in many cases the correlation is not very close. It would appear that the Third World countries may never be able to close the gap between their income and that of the advanced countries because the latter are growing at a rate equal to or higher than the former. Indeed, it is generally agreed that the income gap between advanced and less developed countries has been widening and will probably continue to do so in the future. However, the prospects of closing the gaps in nutrition, health, and even education are much brighter. Finally, if the last two inferences are valid, the Third World countries may be able to achieve substantially higher levels of living without in every case making high scores on an index of income per capita. Some qualitative observations support this conclusion. The United States, for example, is the wealthiest of all nations and spends more for health services per capita than any other country,[3] but many other countries score better on nearly all health indices.[4] The population of the richest countries are not always the best nourished, and it is quite clear that many countries, even with relatively modest income per capita, can achieve high levels of education and culture. Japan is perhaps one of the most notable examples.

The evidence presented above is introduced to make only one point: the wealth and prosperity of nations need not, and indeed should not, be measured by GNP per capita alone. Many other measures would be appropriate, depending on the perspective which people have of national development. The conclusion is obvious: GNP should not be the sole measure of economic growth and national development. But this, of course, does not suggest that it should be ruled out as one of many useful measures.

Admittedly, there is no reliable statistical indicator of levels of human resources development and utilization, and the construction of such a measure would be very difficult. For example, no one has yet devised a comprehensive indicator of human resources *development*. If one were constructed, it should probably include as a minimum: measures of educational achievement, school participation ratios, and numbers and proportions of persons in the labor force with strategic skills (such as artisans, craftsmen, foremen, master farm-

3. Intercountry data on per capita health expenditures are difficult to obtain and are, if available, often not comparable. However, the United States Department of Health, Education and Welfare estimated per capita expenditures on health in the United States to be $238 in 1968. This is clearly much higher than figures in the *World Health Statistics Report* (Vol. 23, No. 11) for a few industrialized nations in the late sixties (converted to United States currency): Canada, $92; West Germany, $109; Sweden, $111; United Kingdom, $92.
4. Among industrial nations, the United States ranks fourteenth in infant mortality, twelfth in maternal mortality, eighteenth in male life expectancy (at birth), and eleventh in female life expectancy (at birth). The death rate for middle-age males is higher than in fifteen other industrial nations. [The Committee for National Health Insurance, *Facts of Life* (Washington, D.C., 1969).]

ers, writers, musicians, teachers, artists, engineers, scientists, administrators, managers). Probably a human resources development indicator should also include a measure of health, and this ideally would include data on life expectancy at various ages, infant mortality, incidence of critical diseases (such as parasites, malaria, and tuberculosis), and availability (that is, geographic distribution) of health services. Finally, some measure of nutrition of the total population, and in particular of very young children, would be useful. However, although the methodology exists to combine various measures of human resources development into a composite index,[5] there is a dearth of reliable data upon which to base them. The measurement of effectiveness of *utilization* of human resources poses even more difficult problems. Not only are data lacking on unemployment, underemployment, or mal-employment (persons working in occupations which do not "fit" their qualifications), but the concepts of measurement themselves still lie beyond the frontiers of present knowledge. Thus, our approach to development and modernization has a major initial handicap. There are as yet no accepted yardsticks for measuring the development and utilization of human resources.

HUMAN RESOURCES PROBLEMS

Human resources problems fall into two general categories: (1) those related to *underdevelopment* of skills, knowledge, and talent of persons in the labor force and (2) those stemming from *underutilization* of their energies and capabilities. These two categories are inter-

5. One particular methodology is described in detail in, Frederick H. Harbison, Joan Maruhnic, and Jane R. Resnick, *Quantitative Analyses of Modernization and Development* (Princeton, N.J.: Industrial Relations Section, Princeton University, 1970). Briefly stated, it is possible, by standardizing values and combining various indicators into one index, to position each one of a group in n-dimensional space. Then the group may be divided into more or less homogeneous subgroups, data may be interpolated or extrapolated, social and economic maturity may be measured by ranking within the group, and goals for planning may be set both in the larger group and/or subgroups. This method is useful for ranking, classifying, and comparing countries or regions within a country with respect to levels of development and modernization.

related. Underdevelopment of human resources is to some extent a cause of underutilization and vice versa.

Almost by definition, a less developed country is one characterized by general underdevelopment of its human resources. A large proportion of the population is illiterate; there are critical shortages of nearly all strategic skills; man's mastery of nature is limited; and, as a consequence, the productivity of the masses is very low. The levels of living of most people in the less developed countries have advanced only slightly, if at all, for centuries largely because of underdevelopment of their skills and knowledge. Human resources policy, therefore, should aim at maximum feasible development of work-oriented capacities of people.

Human skills, knowledge, and work capacities can be developed in many ways. The most obvious is through formal education, beginning at the primary or first level, continuing with one of the various forms of secondary schooling, and then going on to higher education, such as colleges, universities, and technical institutes. Of equal importance is on-the-job development through a wide variety of informal as well as systematic training within the working environment. In addition, individuals develop themselves through reading, independent study, observing and learning from others, and personal experience. Thus, human resources development, or to use a more economically oriented term, "human capital formation," is for most people a lifetime process. It encompasses work-oriented activity in schools, factories, farms, governments, armies, political organization, trade unions, and other institutions. In certain periods and in particular environments human capital formation may be rapid or sluggish. Through time, moreover, human resources embodied in individuals may deteriorate; human capital, like material capital, is subject to depreciation as well as to accumulation.

Underutilization of human resources is likewise characteristic of the developing countries. As will be stressed in the following chapter, the rates of open unemployment in the modern-sector enclaves are generally higher than in the advanced countries. Underemployment or low-productivity employment in subsistence activities is the pervasive state of the masses. Persons with scarce skills are often performing the most menial tasks; specialized talent may be wasted in the wrong kind of activity; and the capacities of the small number of highly educated persons may be depleted in environments offering little incentive or challenge. In short, countries having the most acute shortages of skills are often the ones which utilize them the least effectively.

However, human resources can never be fully or completely developed, for man's capacity for intellectual growth has no upper limit. Nor are human resources ever utilized optimally, for some people will always be unemployed, underemployed, or mal-employed. Even in the most advanced countries, some persons will always be in occupations which underutilize their education, training, or capacity for growth.

As stated above, the problems of underdevelopment and underutilization of human resources are interrelated. Many, though not all, of the problems of underutilization stem from general underdevelopment of human resources. And the drag of rapidly rising rates of population growth exacerbates the problems of both utilization and development.

The problems of human resources underdevelopment can be solved, given sufficient time, energy, and resources. But the problems of underutilization, particularly in countries with high population growth rates, are much more intractable. Both are of central concern to the human resources strategist. In practice, however, he must be satisfied with measures which *improve* development and *improve* utilization by relative standards. The practical goal is maximization of progress, not achievement of utopia.

HUMAN RESOURCES POLICY

Human resources policy can be defined as the constellation of measures or, if it is clearly and consistently formulated, the strategy for grappling with human resources problems. These problems are far-ranging, complex, and interrelated. They stem from no single cause;

their solution requires more than simple remedies. But human resources policy, as such, has seldom been the central concern of economists, planners, educators, politicians, or statesmen. No country has ever attempted to formulate a strategy for optimal development and utilization of its manpower as a goal in itself. There is no core theory which attempts to explain the constellation of processes in the development and utilization of human resources. The reason is obvious: human resources analysis traditionally has been treated as only an element, and a subsidiary one, in analyses from other perspectives. Let us examine this prosposition in greater detail.

Economic policy and planning is centrally concerned with such things as rates of economic growth, income distribution, balance of payments, material capital accumulation, consumption, and investment. From this perspective human agents are evaluated in terms of their contribution to achievement of economic goals. Investment in education, for example, is valued in terms of economic costs and benefits measured by lifetime earnings streams. The broad rationale for developing a country's human resources is to increase national income, and increasing labor productivity is one means to that end. Only rarely is economic policy designed to solve a human resources problem as such.

Perhaps an exception to this rule was the reduction in taxes in the United States in 1965 as a measure designed primarily to lower rates of unemployment by expanding aggregate demand. But subsequently taxes were increased and monetary measures tightened primarily to stem inflation with only secondary consideration to the impact on manpower. Economic policy need not be criticized on this basis; the point to be made is that human resources development and utilization is a subsidiary question—only one of many other factors to be considered in economic policy formulation.

The same is true of *education* policy. Educational theorists and planners are aware that schools, colleges, and universities play a vital role in developing the skills and knowledge needed in the labor force. They might even agree that an additional function of education is to create attitudes and incentives conducive to work. But few educators would accept the notion that the primary function of education is to prepare people for the labor market. For the educator, the more important purpose is to develop man and his intellect as an end in itself, to make him more sensitive to people and things around him, to build consensus on common goals, or in some cases to indoctrinate the young with philosophies of social and political order. The educator is happy to have the support of economists in popularizing the economic value of education, but he will resist the notion that education should be directed solely to economic ends. At the risk of some exaggeration, one might say that the central purpose of education is to increase the demand for and the supply of more education. To the education planner, education has value in itself; it is a human right. To be sure, education may have a great deal to do with human resources development and utilization, but this is a secondary rather than a primary function.

As stressed earlier, human resources are developed as much on the job as in formal education. Employing organizations, therefore, are generators of human skills and knowledge. They may create or destroy incentives for work or develop or ruin human resources. But business enterprises, government ministries, political parties, and armies are not organized for the purpose of development of people. Human resources development is a means—an indispensable element certainly—in building organizations, but organizations have other, more tangible ends. Thus, human resources policy is derived in part from *organizational development* policy, just as it is at the same time a consequence also of *economic* and *education* policies.

There are also human resources aspects of a *welfare* or *poverty* policy. The alleviation of poverty and help for the disadvantaged are important policy objectives. To the extent that such objectives may be achieved by generating employment or providing training, human resources policy is involved. But here again measures designed to develop and utilize human resources are only one means of solving other problems. No welfare or poverty policy is based primarily on human resources considerations.

This analysis can be pursued further. Human resources development is crucial in *science* policy, but here the central objective is the discovery and application of knowledge rather than the development of labor force capacities as such. *Military* policy has a profound impact on human resources, but armies are organized for war and defense rather than for building the skills of people.

In *labor market* policy, to be sure, human resources constitute the primary focus. It is concerned with "matching" men and jobs, with labor mobility, and with terms and conditions of work. It deals also with employment and unemployment. But labor market policy touches only tangentially on education and training in schools and in employing institutions. And when issues of employment generation arise, labor market policy is usually subordinate to general economic policy.

In short, human resources policy is developed in pieces. It is for the most part a consequence of policies formulated in other areas. Almost never has it been the central concern of policy makers. This volume presents another point of view.

The human resources approach is in essence a *perspective* for looking at national development and modernization. It concentrates attention on human resources problems; and it assumes that if these problems can be solved, most of the other obstacles in the path of progress may be removed as a consequence. As stressed throughout the volume, however, the human resources approach is not inconsistent with raising national incomes. Indeed, if followed consistently, it would promote income growth, and in particular it would enable the population as a whole, rather than a privileged few, to share the fruits of progress.

2 | The Underutilization of Human Resources

Without question, underutilization of human resources is the most serious and intractable problem facing the less developed countries today. With very few exceptions, increases in their labor forces, reflecting high rates of population increase, are outpacing the generation of employment opportunities. This is the great tragedy of most of the newly developing countries. Their growth fails to provide opportunities for most of their people and to mobilize their talents and energies in the modernization process. Unfortunately, both the numbers and the proportion of "marginal men" who struggle for survival on the fringes of the urban and rural modern-sector enclaves are increasing. The crucial question is whether appropriate opportunities can be created to utilize effectively a rapidly growing abundance of human resources and thus enable the masses to enjoy some of the fruits of progress.

There are many manifestations of underutilization of human resources. Open unemployment, underemployment, disguised unemployment, or mal-employment are among the more obvious. Moreover, it is difficult to make a distinction between poverty and underutilization. The concepts of employment and unemployment in developing countries are ambiguous and for the most part are different from those applicable to advanced economies. The statistics on various kinds of underutilization are very inadequate. Nevertheless, the problem of underutilization is blindingly obvious: manpower, most abundant of all resources in the developing countries, is grossly

19

underutilized even though it is capable of almost limitless development.

For analytical purposes we can identify three different sectors in the less developed economies—the "modern," the "traditional" (subsistence), and the in-between or "intermediate." The problems of underutilization of human resources are quite different in each.

The modern sector in urban areas includes the small but relatively rich islands or enclaves of economic activity. Here are the larger and more productive manufacturing and commercial enterprises, government ministries and bureaus, major services such as education and public health, communication, public utilities, rail and motor transport, mining, and wholesale trade. Characteristically, this sector employs blue-collar labor for relatively high wages and white-collar employees for high salaries. Entry into this sector is the cherished hope of most members of the labor force. The modern sector includes most of the labor force which is reported in the usual kind of manpower survey.[1]

The subsistence sector in the urban areas is made up of hawkers, stall holders, the ubiquitous shoe-shine boys, intermittent part-time workers, beggars, petty thieves, and others who live in poverty and misery on the periphery of the urban economy. These are the urban "marginal" men and women. In a technical sense they may be "employed," but in reality they are part of the army of the unemployed and underemployed.

Between the modern and subsistence sectors is an intermediate sector which encompasses small family enterprises, retail trade, garages and repair shops, handicrafts, family-type industries, small-scale taxi and lorrie transport, and related activities which for the most part lie beyond the reach of statistical measurement. But this sector is usually quite dynamic; it manufactures for, sells to, and services the bulk of the population. Here wages and incomes are low relative to the modern sector but much higher than in the subsistence sector.

1. Manpower surveys rarely report requirements outside the modern sector since they are usually limited to establishments employing ten or more persons.

Neither the size nor the boundaries of these sectors can be clearly defined, for the distinction between them is more like a gradient than a cliff. In most cases, those attached to the modern sector are a small minority of the urban labor force ranging perhaps from about 5 per cent in most African countries to 20-25 per cent in some of the LDCs in South America and Asia. Like the fringes of a marshy lake, the extent of the subsistence sector is very difficult to chart. It may be assumed that this sector is constantly growing; but it may fluctuate periodically under varying economic and social conditions.

The intermediate sector is also difficult to measure, but in most urban areas it probably employs considerably more persons than the modern sector. This is the sector of small enterprises, indigenous entrepreneurs, and hard-working family groups who manage somehow to live a little bit above the poverty line. At the upper end it merges into the modern sector, and at its lower extremities it is almost indistinguishable from the subsistence sector.

In the rural areas, there are also modern, intermediate, and traditional sectors. The modern sector includes the large plantations with an employed labor force, the larger and more prosperous cash-crop farmers, regional and local government officials, school teachers, and the agents of central governments. The traditional sector consists for the most part of sharecroppers and subsistence farmers largely outside of the monetary economy. And the intermediate sector is made up of small traders, rural craftsmen, some casual workers, and farmers who may produce some crops for cash as well as food for subsistence. Here again there are no sharp distinctions in the continuum between the most modern and the most primitive.

In the developing countries, characteristically, the modern sectors of both urban and rural areas may be growing rapidly and enjoying spectacular prosperity (even though employing very few people), while the others remain almost stagnant. In the modern sectors a minority of the country's work forces may have good jobs and rising levels of living, whereas the masses in the traditional and large numbers in the intermediate continue to live in misery, poverty, and partial idleness. They are bypassed by the country's economic development which is enjoyed by only the privileged few in the modern sectors.

In any of the sectors the dimensions of the problem of under-utilization of human resources are difficult to measure in statistical terms. Open unemployment in urban areas is perhaps the easiest aspect of the problem to measure. It consists of members of the labor force attached to the modern or intermediate sectors who are presumably looking for and unable to find wage employment, as well as those who may be seeking some sort of reasonably lucrative self-employ-ment. Expressed as a proportion of a country's *total* labor force, open unemployment rates are relatively low, ranging perhaps from 2 or 3 to 5 or 6 per cent. (In a few exceptional cases, for example, Ceylon, it may go as high as 15 per cent.) But as a *proportion of the urban labor force,* the rates are more likely to be from 10 to 25 per cent. In nearly all of the LDCs these rates appear to be rising. Ac-cording to a study of available statistics compiled by Turnham,[2] rates of open unemployment in the LDCs are higher than in the advanced countries, and they are especially high for younger workers. He fur-ther shows that these rates are high *despite* great difficulties in meas-urement and, that with labor forces growing at 2 to 3 per cent a year, even a constant percentage rate of unemployment implies a consider-able annual growth in the number of unemployed. According to the more pessimistic view of Singer, unemployment in the LDCs is al-ready close to 20 to 25 per cent of the labor force as compared with 3 to 5 per cent in the rich countries and will continue to increase unless counter-influencing trends appear.[3] An exhaustive survey of employment in Colombia, conducted by the ILO,[4] concluded that

2. David Turnham, *The Employment Problem in Less Developed Countries* (Paris: Organization for Economic Cooperation and Development, Develop-ment Centre, June 1970), pp. 56-57.
3. H. W. Singer, "International Policies and Their Effect on Employment," Cambridge Conference on Development Problems, 7th, 1970, *Prospects for Employment Opportunity in the Nineteen Seventies,* edited by Ronald Robin-son and Peter Johnston (London: H.M. Stationery Office, 1971), pp. 194-202.
4. International Labour Office, *Towards Full Employment, op. cit.,* Chap. 3.

about 25 per cent of the urban labor force suffered from a lack of work opportunities in 1967. It also estimated that the active labor force was growing at a rate of 3½ per cent annually, whereas modern-sector employment was expanding by only 2 to 2½ per cent and, if these trends were to continue, more than one-third of the labor force would be unemployed by 1985. David Morse, formerly Director-General of the ILO, has claimed that there may be as many as 75 million persons unemployed in the Third World.[5] Logically, one should add underemployment to open unemployment figures. This would include those working only part time who would prefer to be employed full time. In most cases, however, it is difficult to ascertain whether or not they are included in the available unemployed estimates.

Open unemployment and underemployment in the cities, however, is only the exposed portion of the iceberg of underutilization. Those in the traditional sector, who are underemployed in the sense that they neither produce nor earn enough to rise above minimum subsistence levels, are seldom included in the statistical estimates, nor are the masses of subsistence farmers, sharecroppers, and others in the rural areas who are outside the monetized economy. Indeed, in the subsistence sectors, as well as in the lower ranks of the intermediate, the problems of underemployment and poverty are indistinguishable. People are poor because of lack of opportunity, skills, and capacity to raise their levels of living. In order to increase their income, it is necessary to increase their productivity, that is, to utilize them more effectively. For this group, the true measure of underutilization, therefore, may not be the extent of employment but rather the levels of real income (in kind or cash) which human activity generates.

There are thus many concepts of unemployment and underemployment as applied to developing countries, and there is no generally accepted definition. As Myrdal has noted, the term "underemploy-

5. David A. Morse, "The Employment Problem in Developing Countries," Cambridge Conference on Development Problems, 7th, 1970, *Prospects for Employment Opportunities in the Nineteen Seventies, op. cit.,* pp. 5-13.

ment" and its many synonyms—"hidden," "concealed," "invisible," "disguised," "potential," and "latent" unemployment—are used with considerable variation of meaning by various writers. Basically, however, these terms all represent an attempt to state the fact that the labor force actually engaged in a certain type of economic activity is idle during part of the day, week, month, and year, or, if working, is "unproductive."[6] Others including Thorbecke and Stoutjesdijk have concentrated on underemployment in agriculture. Here they use the concept of "effective employment rate" which is defined as the ratio (expressed as a percentage) of the man-days required to produce the total output to the available man-days over the course of years. Using this concept, they conclude, for example, that effective employment in Peru and Guatemala amounted, respectively, to only 57 and 70 per cent of economically active population in agriculture in 1965.[7] Economists and others are making determined efforts to improve the quantitative measurement of unemployment and underemployment. Yet finding solutions for the problem need not wait for such refinements. Human resources policy in the LDCs must direct itself not only to open unemployment but also to the much larger, more pervasive, and less measurable underutilization of the masses of low-income, low-productivity members of the active population. Clearly, the anatomy of underutilization of human resources in the LDCs bears little resemblance to that of unemployment as defined in the advanced countries.

In sizing up the problems, we can agree with the following assessment by Robert S. McNamara in September 1971.

Today, I believe most economists would agree that:

Unemployment and underemployment are extremely serious in the developing countries, much more so than in the developed countries.

6. For a critical appraisal of the concept and theory of underemployment, see Gunnar Myrdal, *Asian Drama* (New York: Twentieth Century Fund, 1968), Vol. III, Appendix 6, pp. 2041-61.
7. E. Thorbecke and E. Stoutjesdijk, *Employment and Output—A Methodology Applied to Peru and Guatemala* (Paris: Organization for Economic Cooperation and Development, Development Centre, 1971). See in particular Chap. V, pp. 131-48.

On reasonable definitions—including allowances for underemployment—unemployment approximates 20-25 percent in most countries.
If past patterns continue, unemployment is bound to become worse.[8]

In this chapter we examine the possible avenues for improvement of utilization of human resources, first in the urban and later in the rural areas. And in Chapters 3 and 5 we look at still another manifestation of underutilization—mal-employment.[9]

UNDERUTILIZATION IN URBAN AREAS—SOME POSSIBLE REMEDIES

The genesis of open unemployment and underemployment in the cities is simple: the actual and potential urban labor force grows much more rapidly than employment opportunities. The high rate of expansion of the labor force is largely the consequence of generally high rates of population growth magnified by widespread rural-urban migration. Nearly all cities in the Third World face this dilemma. And with population rates on the rise in most countries, the volume of unemployment in the cities is almost certain to increase at least for the next several decades. Even under very optimistic estimates of increases in GNP, the maximum annual growth of new job generation in urban areas is not likely to exceed 6 or 7 per cent; a more likely estimate would be about half that rate; and in many cases modern-sector employment is hardly growing at all. In contrast, the rate of increase in urban labor forces is usually about twice the general rate of increase of population and/or national labor force. Thus, in

8. Robert S. McNamara, Address to the Board of Governors, International Bank for Reconstruction and Development, p. 7, Washington, D.C., September 27, 1971.
9. In this case, human resources are poorly utilized in terms of their skills. For example, university graduates may be employed in occupations requiring little more than secondary education; engineers may be employed beneath their skills as draftsmen; highly trained scientists may be relegated to teaching elementary courses in secondary schools. Such mal-employment is common in nearly all developing countries despite critical shortages of strategic skills. For the most part, mal-employment is the consequence of poor co-ordination between a country's employment and education systems. It is confined largely to the modern sector and involves relatively small numbers of people. And, as explained more fully in Chapter 5, it is a major cause of the brain drain from the less developed countries.

countries with population increases of 2½ to 3 per cent per year, the annual increase in urban labor forces may range as high as 6 to 7 per cent. With few exceptions, therefore, urban unemployment and underemployment are bound to increase.

The obvious approaches to cope with this problem are, first, to increase the employment-generating capacity of the urban areas and, second, to stem the expansion of urban labor forces. Both are extremely difficult.

In the manufacturing sector, jobs may be increased by influencing *how* products are made (that is, use of more labor-intensive technology) and by influencing *what* products are made (for example, through promoting consumer expenditures on goods which require more labor rather than capital or foreign exchange).

A cogent argument can be made that the use of more labor-intensive technologies in manufacturing establishments may generate more jobs in the modern sector. This may be achieved by more realistic factor-pricing through changing overvalued exchange rates and other financial policies which tend to subsidize the importation of expensive capital equipment, thereby artificially reducing the cost of capital relative to labor. The first step would be to raise the price of capital imports by devaluating exchange rates, raising interest rates, and discontinuing subsidies and other forms of encouragement to purchase capital-intensive machinery. Though feasible in many cases, the extent of possible employment generation by such means is very limited. It is questionable, in the first place, whether there is a wide range of choice in the selection of technology for many modern-sector manufacturing enterprises. Machinery must be imported from advanced countries where labor-saving rather than labor-using processes are the major concern. More important, however, the arbitrary selection of more labor-intensive technology may seriously jeopardize the long-range objective of manufacturing enterprises in some developing countries to sell their products in international markets. Finally, since the total employment in modern manufacturing is so low anyway (in most African countries it would not amount to more than 2 or 3 per cent of the labor force at best, and in the more advanced Latin American or Asian countries certainly not more than 6 to 8 per cent), the resulting increase in new jobs, even if all feasible labor-intensive technologies were utilized, would be minimal.

The possibilities of employment generation through expansion of the intermediate sector are probably much greater. This sector is already more labor-intensive, and it could be modernized and expanded through greater use of appropriate technology to make small industries more productive with minimum inputs of capital,[10] but it very likely would not be profitable under existing factor-pricing. In any case, at present most developing countries are short of know-how and determination to develop and apply such technology. Local scientists and engineers, steeped in knowledge about the latest technologies of advanced countries, show little interest in it, and research organizations in the advanced countries see little profit in studying and developing it. Even where such technologies may be available, the delivery systems for their application are as yet undeveloped. Thus, the expansion and modernization of the intermediate sector is a long-range undertaking which is only tentatively begun in few countries. It will require rather sweeping changes in the curriculum, orientation, and instruction provided in university faculties of science and engineering and in the technical colleges. It calls for establishment of new research and development organizations within the developing countries. It will involve a generation of new cadres of entrepreneurs and managers which are not now being produced in the schools or

---

10. [Appropriate] technology might be interpreted, wrongly, to mean that the latest or best techniques are too good for the newly developing countries. . . . The true point is that these countries need to select from the entire world reservoir of scientific and technological ideas . . . which are *best suited to their structures of resources and needs.* . . . In many fields further inventions are needed—new equipment designs, for example, specially tailored to the capital-scarce, labor-surplus, small-market conditions of many newly developing countries. Such new industrial technologies, which would be both *modern* and *appropriate,* can be developed by . . . analyzing the technological problems of the newly developing countries directly, to come up with novel approaches through fresh research and development. See Eugene Staley and Richard Morse, *Modern Small Industry for Developing Countries* (New York: McGraw-Hill, 1965), p. 288.

training centers or institutions of higher education. It will require the building of many more extension services, parallel to those in agriculture, to promote and guide the application of new technologies once they are developed.

Considerable employment could be generated by providing encouragement and even subsidies for the manufacture of goods for export. In the case of most developing countries, this would mean concentrating their efforts on small and intermediate sized enterprises which are by nature relatively labor-intensive. Products such as plywood, simple textiles, component parts for radio, television, and other electronic equipment, specialties such as wigs, and many handicraft products are good examples. Indeed, as emphasized later in this chapter,* exports of such labor-intensive products have been a major source of both income growth and employment generation in Taiwan and Korea. This kind of "outward-looking" strategy of industrial development as opposed to an "inward-looking" strategy of encouragement of capital-intensive import substitution industries may have great potential for employment generation. But it is dependent upon building aggressive entrepreneurship—particularly in small and medium sized enterprises, the existence of reasonable wage levels in relation to investment costs, and very deliberate efforts on the part of government to restrict the availability of capital for expensive import-substitution projects. Such a policy, however, is not likely to appeal to government leaders who are impressed by the trappings of modern industrialization such as steel mills, petroleum refineries, automobile assembly plants, and beer or soft drink bottling facilities. Some countries, of course, which have rich mineral resources, are outward-looking in exporting petroleum products and processed mineral ores, but these activities do not normally generate much employment. The big potential generators of employment opportunities are much more likely to be the smaller and less glamorous enterprises which can rely on innovative technology and relatively cheap labor. Here the intermediate sector, rather than the modern, is likely to have the comparative advantage in employment generation.

* See pp. 45-49.

In all urban areas, construction has a good deal of potential for employment generation. It is, or easily can be, a labor-intensive activity, and it offers perhaps the widest range of possibilities for substitution of men for machines. And in many developing countries construction employs more persons than manufacturing, and thus the increment to employment from its expansion is potentially larger. Thus, massive investments in building roads, sewers, water supplies, apartments, and urban housing of all kinds, using relatively labor-intensive techniques, have considerable employment-generation potential. However, the major question here, as also will be discussed later, is whether such investments would be better concentrated in the rural rather than the urban areas.

The expansion of public services, together with restraint on introduction of labor-saving machinery in government offices, could create additional employment, since government is such a large employer in the urban areas in most of the developing countries. Yet budget stringencies, as well as understandable reluctance to "make work" for more persons in already overstaffed bureaucracies argue against such measures. Perhaps the most promising possibilities lie in the extension and improvement of education and public health, both of which are big and very labor-intensive activities. And both provide services of high priority for developing countries.

Another possible means of employment generation is to break skill bottlenecks in both the intermediate and modern sectors. This is a popular notion with planners and educators alike. Jobs may be waiting for engineers, scientists, and doctors; positions for technicians and skilled craftsmen are available if they are willing to work for the wages offered; competent managerial and supervisory personnel are always in short supply. The breaking of such skill bottlenecks might lead to greater employment of the unskilled. For the most part, however, the possible multiplier effects of breaking skill bottlenecks have yet to be explored. And although the need for more skilled workers is self-evident, the effective demand for their services in terms of actual openings at specified wages has seldom been determined with any accuracy. Here is a problem area in which research is urgently needed and where the returns, in terms of guidelines for human resources development policy, could be great indeed.

Many other measures of employment generation can be mentioned. Shorter workdays or workweeks, reduction of overtime, and elimination of restrictions (such as rules limiting layoffs and discharges) are frequently advocated. Another approach is simply to require employers to hire more workers than they need. For example, in Kenya on two separate occasions, in 1964 and 1970, an attempt was made to create more jobs by requiring all enterprises, both public and private, to expand employment by arbitrarily stated amounts. These measures, however, more often than not turn out to be counter-productive.

A final major consideration is incomes policy through wage restraint. Relatively high wages and salaries in the modern sector, in the view of most economists, provide incentives for use of labor-saving technologies. At the same time high wages act as a magnet drawing more people from rural areas in the hope of finding lucrative jobs. Wage restraint would serve a dual purpose: it might increase employment, and it could help to stem migration by reducing the income gap between rural and urban areas.

In a recent paper on unemployment in Africa, Charles Frank offers evidence in support of this thesis.[11] Actually, reductions in real wages in the modern sector have been made in some African countries. In Tanzania there have been cuts in the salaries of higher civil servants. In Ghana and Sierra Leone, real wages have been held down both through restraint in increasing money wages and the effects of inflation. In Kenya, a recent decree (spring 1970) for a 10 per cent across-the-board increase in employment was coupled with suspension of annual increments in the salaries of government workers. Frank shows that during the last two decades there has been a significant negative association between rises in real wages and growth of employment in several African countries. As he points out:

11. Charles R. Frank, Jr., *The Problem of Urban Unemployment in Africa* (Princeton, N.J.: Princeton University, Woodrow Wilson School, Research Program in Economic Development), Discussion Paper No. 16, p. 7.

Ghana, in which real wages have fallen by more than 7 percent, has experienced the most rapid growth in employment. In Sierra Leone growth in real wages has been moderate and employment has increased at a rapid pace. Where real wages have increased very rapidly in the fifties and sixties as in Kenya, Uganda, and Tanzania, employment opportunities have been virtually stagnant.[12]

And Elliot J. Berg, in a paper presented in Cambridge, England, to representatives of the less developed countries, claims that there is a consensus—shared by observers of very different ideological and political persuasions—that wage restraint is in order in most of the less developed countries.[13]

Although economists may agree on a wage restraint policy, it is not likely to be popular among civil servants, trade unionists, and other well-positioned members of the modern-sector labor forces of the developing countries. It will be difficult to persuade this small but powerful minority, who only recently have begun to enjoy the fruits of modernization, that their wages and salaries are already too high and rising too rapidly. Yet the developing countries will be forced to face this issue, and here extensive research could be of critical importance.

In summary, there are many conceivable ways of expanding employment opportunities in urban areas, but none are easy. The substitution of labor-intensive technology in existing modern-sector manufacturing enterprises offers little promise for substantial employment generation. The modernization of the intermediate sectors would expand employment, but this is likely to be a slow process. In the modern and particularly the intermediate sectors, a policy of promotion of labor-intensive manufacturing for export, coupled with discouragement of capital-intensive import-substitution industries, has greater potential if governments are prepared to take the required measures. Construction and investment in public works can be used to generate jobs; and the provision of essential government services such as education and improved public health would undoubtedly

12. *Ibid.*, p. 21.
13. Elliot J. Berg, "Wages Policy and Employment in Less Developed Countries," Cambridge Conference on Development Problems, 7th, 1970, *Prospects for Employment Opportunities in the Nineteen Seventies, op. cit.,* pp. 95-107.

expand employment opportunities. Employment generation could further be stimulated by restriction of imports consumed mostly by the rich and the promotion of local production of "wage goods" such as food products, clothing, low-cost housing, bicycles, and inexpensive furniture. All of these measures are likely to be facilitated if the rise in wages and salaries can be restrained, and all could be frustrated by trade unions, organizations of civil servants, and politicians pressing for very substantial increases in the pay of their constituents.

Yet, even if more employment could be generated in the cities through application of an effective combination of the many measures mentioned above, the problem of rising urban unemployment would still be far from solved, and indeed it might even be aggravated. Unfortunately, as more jobs become available in the urban modern sectors, more job seekers are likely to migrate from the rural areas because of the greater probability of finding employment.[14] In a sense, the rural-urban migration is the result of a sort of "gold rush" fever. Many seek rewards which few are successful in finding. The lure of high wages and the opportunity to participate in the fruits of modernization make it worthwhile for many persons, particularly the younger and better educated, to take a chance on finding work in the urban areas. The possibility of staying with relatives or fellow tribesmen already in the cities makes subsistence easier while searching for the magic opportunity. For the few who succeed, the rewards of high wages and permanent employment are very great indeed. But these hopeful job seekers in the meantime swell the ranks of the intermediate sector, augmenting underemployment and depressing wages if, indeed, they rise out of the subsistence sector. The provision of low-cost housing, better education, and improved welfare services for the urban population only exacerbate the problem by providing additional incentives for migration.

More jobs and better living conditions in the cities, therefore, generate a greater supply of job seekers. The expansion of employment

14. For elaboration of this thesis, see J. R. Harris and M. P. Todaro, "Migration, Unemployment, and Development: A Two-Sector Analysis," *American Economic Review,* Vol. LX, No. 1 (March 1970), pp. 126-42.

in the cities is likely to be a major cause rather than a cure of unemployment. Can the supply of urban labor be restricted? To use an
aviation phrase, is there some way of devising a sort of "holding
pattern" to stem the surge of hopeful job seekers into the cities?

Theoretically, the supply of labor to the cities may be restricted in
several ways, but some are impractical and others would be ruled out
on humanitarian grounds. For example, the Tanzanian government,
on occasion, has attempted to round up unemployed migrants in Dar
es Salaam and return them to rural areas by lorry. This is at best
temporarily effective. Exhortation by high officials for job seekers to
remain in the countryside is almost never successful. Emphasizing the
virtues of rural life through changes in the school curriculum is not
likely to fool either parents or their youngsters who desire escape
from the bush. Countries could, of course, curtail education in the
rural areas since it tends to excite the aspirations of the young to find
urban employment. Or, since many immigrants go to the cities in
search of secondary, vocational, and higher education which may be
nonexistent in the rural areas, school places in the cities could be
allocated by residency requirements. But such measures are so repug-
nant on humanistic grounds that they would be rejected out of hand
by responsible political leaders.

Another possibility might be to put larger numbers of young men
and women into the armed forces. Arguments in favor of this idea
would be that wages might be held at relatively low levels, skills relevant to civilian employment could be developed, and respect for order
and discipline might be encouraged. The counter-arguments are obvious and, in addition, few commanders would accept happily the idea
of transforming the military into an employment-generating and skill-
building force. Yet in some cases it may be necessary to retain young
people in the military if no civilian jobs are available to them. Unfortunately, Nigeria faced this problem in the early seventies. To de-
mobilize its forces recruited during the civil war of the late sixties
without provision of employment opportunities would augment urban
unemployment which was dangerously high. To organize civilian
youth brigades would be expensive and perhaps politically hazard-

ous. Thus, retention in the armed forces offered the best of admittedly bleak alternatives.

Another solution often recommended is to keep young people in school longer and to retire older workers earlier. This may follow logically as more opportunities for secondary and higher education are created, but few economists or politicians would argue for a policy *primarily* designed to keep young people out of the labor force by compulsory schooling.

A system of national service for all youth is often advocated both on grounds of creating jobs for a one- or two-year period of service as well as keeping young people temporarily out of the urban labor force. The problem here is not only the expense of such a project but more critically the organization and direction of it. The task of building a universal national youth service and directing its activities exceeds the capacities even of most advanced countries. Progress is being made, however, in organizing national service programs on a limited scale in many African countries, and further investigation, research, and experimentation would certainly appear to be appropriate.

Regardless of the success of any combination of these approaches, the conclusion is inescapable that the two most effective ways of limiting the increase in urban labor forces are population limitation, which is a very long-range solution, and retention of surplus labor in the rural areas, which offers the best short-range solution. It may be somewhat easier to retain people in rural areas if wage and salary increases can be restrained in the cities. But to assume that labor may willingly remain in the countryside in subsistence agriculture and related activities is unrealistic. The rural areas can provide "holding patterns" for surplus labor only if they can provide higher incomes and more abundant opportunities for the rural population.

RURAL DEVELOPMENT

In most of the developing countries the rural population and labor force are destined to increase in absolute numbers for the next several decades and, in some countries with very high population increase rates, they may rise in proportion as well. The United Nations has estimated that 97 per cent of the projected increases in rural and small-town population during the period 1960-80 will take place in the less developed countries. In this period there will be an increase of 645 million rural dwellers in these countries. And of 63 million new members of the labor force in India alone during the next decade, 47 million are expected to need jobs in rural areas. In Latin America, about one-third of the net increase in population will have to remain in agriculture for the next two or three decades. Indeed, in the next decade the Latin American agricultural labor force is expected to increase at twice the average rate of 1950-68, or by nearly a million members per year.[15] It is clear, therefore, that in terms of sheer numbers the most serious problems of underutilization in Third World countries will be experienced in the rural sector. Thus, rural development is essential to provide higher levels of living for the rural masses. It is also essential to stem the flow of migrants to the cities where employment opportunities are quite limited. In other words, the solution for mounting unemployment in the cities will depend in large measure upon the expansion of opportunities in the countryside.

At this point, the term "rural development" should be defined. It encompasses much more than an increase in agricultural and live-stock output and productivity. Village and small town development, extension of health and education services, expansion of local trade and commerce, organization of co-operatives, the provision of credit, the creation of local industries for processing agricultural products, and the improvement of housing, water supplies, sanitation, roads, and communications are all within its scope. It necessitates investment in many kinds of rural public works in addition to those required for improvement of agriculture as such. Broadly based rural development means the transformation of stagnant, traditional societies into productive, dynamic rural economies.

15. These estimates are reported in Robert d'A. Shaw, *Jobs and Agricultural Development* (Washington: Overseas Development Council, 1970), pp. 4-5.

The logic in favor of rural development is clear. It will help solve the problems of hunger and malnutrition; it can ease pressure on the balance of payments by reducing the need to import food; by increasing rural incomes, it will broaden the market for urban produced goods. And above all, since by nature most activities essential to rural development are relatively labor-intensive, it can be a powerful force for generating employment.

In the sixties, it appeared that there might be a collision between population growth and food production. There were dire predictions that the developing countries would be unable to feed themselves in the decades ahead. But this worry is now being dispelled by the discovery of dramatic new technologies designed to increase agricultural output. As Lester Brown implies in *The Seeds of Change,*[16] Americans may feel that the moon landing by the astronauts is the outstanding technical achievement of this generation but, for one billion Asians for whom rice is the staple food, the development of "IR-8" and its dissemination throughout Asia is a much more meaningful accomplishment. From a purely technical standpoint, many economists now agree that the Green Revolution may be able to solve the problem of food production at least for the next two or three decades.

In the next few decades, however, the *means* of production and distribution of food and the *means* of generating opportunities for the masses to share some of the fruits of progress are likely to be the more dominant concerns. Employment generation rather than simple aggregate production is the crucial problem. The new technologies of food production in themselves will not solve the problems of underemployment and income disparities. Indeed, unless managed carefully, they may displace millions of rural workers and push them in even greater numbers into the already overcrowded cities. They could magnify the disparities between the rich and the poor in the rural areas which would make development even more meaningless for the masses than it has been in recent years.

The new wheat and rice growing technology, to be sure, is quite

16. Lester R. Brown, *The Seeds of Change* (New York: Praeger, 1970).

labor-intensive. It requires extensive inputs of labor on irrigation, weed and pest control, fertilizer, and cultivation. Labor inputs per acre are greater. But the larger and more prosperous farmers, who already belong to the rural modern sector, are in the best position to use the new technology. They have better access to technical assistance, credit, and marketing organizations; they are better equipped to manage the necessary inputs; and they have greater political power in local affairs. And as they prosper from use of the new technology, they may acquire more land and also purchase labor-displacing machinery. As the prices for wheat and rice fall as a consequence of greatly expanded production, the smallholder using the traditional methods can be placed at a great disadvantage. And as machines replace men, more sharecroppers may lose their opportunity to make a living on the land. The new technologies and the miracle seeds, therefore, may result in rapid growth of rural modern-sector enclaves, benefiting the large landowners and farmers while increasing the income disparities between the rich and the poor in the rural areas.

The dilemma of the Green Revolution is well summarized by Robert Shaw in his recent monograph:

The Green Revolution brings opportunities for raising productivity among farmers, for intensifying and diversifying agriculture, for giving governments more flexibility in their pursuit of development, and hence creating more jobs. It brings hope to the majority of the world's poor. But the opportunities are mixed with danger—the threats of growing inequalities between rich and poor farmers, of men being replaced by machines before other jobs are available to them, and of some regions outpacing others in development. It should be stressed that the essence of the Green Revolution is simply the creation of a superior agricultural technology. But the *effects* of this technology on society will depend upon the policies and institutions that implement it.[17]

Among the most essential elements in a strategy of rural employment generation are the following:[18]

17. Robert d'A. Shaw, *op. cit.,* p. 70.
18. A much more thorough and comprehensive discussion of an employment generation strategy for agriculture is presented in Shaw, *ibid.,* particularly pp. 55-71.

1. the use of productive but labor-intensive technology;
2. encouragement of smallholder farms;
3. land reform coupled with technical and financial assistance to new owners;
4. encouragement of rurally based industries and commercial enterprises;
5. investment in rural public works and public services;
6. assistance to farmers in the subsistence sector;
7. development of the institutions and administrative capacity for implementation of rural development programs.

The needless mechanization of agriculture may generate unemployment and poverty in rural areas. As in the case of machinery for capital-intensive industry in the modern urban sectors, many less developed countries subsidize, through favorable exchange arrangements, low interest rates, and other means, the importation of large tractors and combines. Intermediate labor-using machines in many cases are unavailable or are unprofitable because of the pricing policies already mentioned. The sophisticated implements made in advanced countries to overcome labor shortages have strong appeal to large farmers in the developing countries who often are quite eager to free themselves of the nuisance of hiring more hands. The temptation to use capital-intensive machinery is further increased by aid-giving countries which have an interest in expanding markets for their industries. As a general rule, subsidies of all kinds on labor-saving agricultural machinery should be eliminated. At the very least, the full costs of such machinery should be paid by the farmers using it, and in many cases it could be subject to heavy taxation. But machinery-limitation policies must be selective. In some situations, higher yields per acre and more intensive land use, for example in multiple cropping, may be dependent upon mechanization. And there are cases where the judicious use of labor-saving machinery may actually be the means of generating employment. Clearly, a viable mechanization policy for agriculture would have to stem from extensive research on the employment-generation consequences of the use of various kinds of machinery in particular situations.

If the Green Revolution and similar technological advances are to generate rather than reduce employment, the number of small, self-employed farmers should be expanded at the expense of the larger landholders. There seems to be abundant evidence that small free-holders, provided they have access to technical help and credit, are likely to work their holdings more intensively than large farmers, and they are much less inclined to use labor-saving machinery. Thus, a policy of limiting the size of landholdings coupled with programs of assistance to small farmers could be a major means of employment generation.

Land reform, of course, is in many countries a necessary measure for limiting large holdings and providing opportunities for smal free-holders. But land reform by itself will do little to improve levels of living. The new owners must be provided with a variety of services—technical assistance, credit and marketing services, adequate water supplies, and the like—and these may involve great expenditure of both financial and human resources.

The development of rurally based industries and commercial services will promote off-farm employment in rural areas. To some extent, non-farm rural enterprises will expand because of the "multiplier" effect of increases in farm incomes. But in some cases governments may have to take specific measures to encourage investment in food-processing industries in the rural areas as opposed to urban centers.

Investment in rural public works and expansion of public services such as schooling, training, and public health have great potential. Large numbers of underemployed peasants, sharecroppers, and rural village dwellers can be constructively engaged in building access roads, digging irrigation canals, constructing schools and health centers, and improving water supplies and sanitation facilities. As long as food production is increasing, some of the payment for public works could be in kind (food and other necessities) as well as in cash. There is also great scope for self-help projects. Public works designed simply to create jobs, however, could be counter-productive unless they are effectively geared to the essential needs of the rural infrastructure. Similarly, the extension of schooling, training programs, and health services should be geared to the essential requirements for development of local communities.

In most countries, however, a rural public works program of sufficient magnitude to generate really significant increases in employment would require rather fundamental shifting of investment priorities from urban to rural emphasis. Because of resource constraints, planners would have to favor rural works over more boulevards, apartments, hotels, schools, public buildings, and other amenities in the cities. At the same time the tax burden of urban dwellers would have to be maintained if not increased. Such measures would certainly engender strong opposition from those already well established in the urban modern sectors who are likely also to wield great political power. However, if rural development proceeds, the masses in those areas would be paying some of the costs from their increased incomes.

The improvement in levels of living and in utilization of human resources in rural subsistence farming, though usually neglected by planners, is fully as important as increasing output and employment in the modern sector. For years to come, many country dwellers are likely to live largely outside of the monetary economy. But their levels of subsistence may be increased by producing more and better food, improving shelter and homemade clothing, providing basic education and minimal health services. In other words they can produce and consume more—that is, utilize their energies better—without increasing their monetary income. Subsistence farmers, however, are difficult to reach and hard to motivate; of all groups they are perhaps the most resistant to change. The inputs of trained extension workers, teachers, and medical personnel are likely to result in much greater costs of assistance per individual serviced than those provided to the modern sector. But if improvement in development and utilization of *all* human resources is a major objective of development policy, these people must not be neglected.

The measures described above have potential for expanding the incomes and broadening the opportunities of rural populations. But to be effective, they must be employed in combination. The organization of an integrated rural development effort, however, is the most complex and critical task of all, and the range of effort required is vast. In agriculture it requires encouragement of and assistance to small freeholders in producing cash crops; it calls for tangible improvement in subsistence food production for many outside the money economy; in many countries it will necessitate sweeping land reform, as well as imaginative programs to motivate peasants numbed for decades by despair and stagnation. The sheer physical task of reaching the masses rather than the few who are better off and more receptive to innovation is an undertaking of staggering proportions. And beyond the task of organization of the production of food are the equally baffling problems of organizing distribution, marketing, credit, transportation, and communication.

Paradoxically, it is relatively easy for the developing countries to build the institutions for modern industrialization. Here the inputs of skills, the appropriate training, and the required organizational architecture are all fairly well known, and the scarce components can be imported from the advanced countries. But for massive rural development, the skills are uncertain, the organizational structures are not developed, the leadership is unidentified, and the techniques for motivating change are largely unexplored. Both with respect to theory and practice, organization for rural transformation is probably the most underdeveloped area of knowledge in the entire field of economic growth.

In conclusion, there are a number of measures which, if taken in combination, could greatly improve the utilization of the expanding rural labor forces. Levels of living in the countryside can be raised, and the rural-urban migration of hopeful job seekers could be stemmed at least in part. But these measures require, in most cases, some reordering of priorities. It cannot be assumed that a policy of maximizing the gross product of the agricultural sector will lead to the most effective utilization of rural manpower. An integrated strategy for expansion of rural employment, in addition to changing priorities in investment, will depend upon sweeping improvements in organizational and administrative capacity in rural areas. This is the point of greatest weakness in most of the developing countries. Here is an example of where the effective utilization of human resources depends upon the development of persons with strategic skills, knowledge, and capacity. This will be discussed more fully in the chapters to follow.

We have identified a wide range of measures for improving the utilization of human resources in the developing countries. All have been mentioned repeatedly by other writers. All will face opposition from powerful forces; and none, taken by itself, would be very effective. At this point two conclusions seem obvious: first, the remedies for underutilization of human resources must be found in employment generation in *both* the rural and urban sectors, through appropriate industrialization as well as through far-reaching rural transformation; second, such employment generation will require a combination of measures, or more precisely a strategy which integrates many actions on different fronts, all directed at the principal target of employment generation. Is it possible, then, to formulate a strategy to achieve full employment? And if so, would such a strategy be consistent with simultaneous achievement of higher levels of national income? There is reason to answer both questions in the affirmative.

EMPLOYMENT-ORIENTED DEVELOPMENT STRATEGIES:
SOME CASES

The ILO report, *Towards Full Employment,* is the first attempt to draw up a comprehensive employment-oriented strategy for development.[19] On a sector-by-sector basis it examines all possible measures for employment generation. It identifies areas such as land reform where basic structural changes are required. It explores and advo-

19. International Labour Office, *Towards Full Employment, op. cit.*

cates most of the approaches to utilization of human resources examined in this chapter and suggests others which have particular significance for Colombia. It establishes sectoral employment targets and assesses the possibilities and difficulties in meeting them. It concludes that employment opportunities must be generated in both urban and rural areas, and in industry, commerce, and public works, as well as in agriculture and related rural activities. The expected consequence of this multifaceted program for fuller utilization of human resources is an overall annual rate of growth in GNP in excess of 8 per cent, a figure higher than ever before achieved by Colombia. The goal of the Colombia proposal is to create 5 million new jobs by 1985, and the strategy for attaining it is a "package" of policies which must fit together as the following summary statement indicates.

We would emphasise that this strategy is a "package" of policies which fit together. A big investment programme would provide the infrastructure needed; it would also give an impetus to the growth of incomes and thus to the demand for goods produced by the private sector. Higher taxation is needed to provide resources for both the capital and the current elements in this programme, as well as for limiting the demand for consumer durables which are capital-intensive. Incomes policy could encourage the search for labour-intensive techniques; it could also reduce the attractiveness of the cities. Unless an over-valued exchange rate is avoided, it will be very hard to carry through the necessary export drive or to prevent a continued over-mechanisation of output. Faster agricultural growth is necessary to meet the demand for food, to earn foreign exchange and also to provide the markets needed for industrial products. Land reform is, on the one hand, needed to absorb some of the growth in the labour force in productive employment; on the other, it is an additional way of limiting the expenditure of the rich. Increased educational expenditure is needed to provide the skills which are necessary, as well as an understanding of the country's problems; it would also provide jobs for unemployed teachers and reduce the numbers looking for work in the younger age group, where unemployment is particularly heavy. Better health services would not merely be desirable in themselves; they would improve the quality of the labour force and help to provide the framework for a policy of population limitation. The provision of social services in country areas, especially for education and health, is a condition for inducing people to settle on new land and thus for the increased agricultural output required.

These policies are all needed together if the 5 million jobs are to be provided. The exact "mix" might of course be varied. A rather faster pace of
land reform, for example, would reduce the burden on the rest of the economy. But a programme broadly of this shape and on this scale seems necessary. To dispense with any major part of it would make the attainment of
full employment in this century highly unlikely.[20]

If adopted as a whole, sufficient income growth is envisioned to
permit the great mass rather than a tiny minority of Colombians to
become much better off and, in concentrating on generation of employment opportunities, to provide special benefits for those population groups who have been least able to share in the fruits of past
progress. The strategy thus strikes directly at income distribution
which is assumed to be consistent with as well as a propelling force
for greater income generation.

The second ILO country study, *Matching Employment Opportunities and Expectations,* outlines a parallel employment-oriented development strategy for Ceylon.[21] The problems are, if anything, more
acute than those in Colombia. Here the authors identify and discuss
in detail four main factors in the crisis in Ceylon: high rates of population increase, balance-of-payment difficulties caused by insuffi-
ciency of exports, an educational system wholly out of gear with the
manpower requirements of the country, and government policy inertia. The problem of mass unemployment, though formidable by any
standard, is particularly serious with jobless secondary school leavers.
There is also widespread underemployment and/or mal-employment
as evidenced by those working short hours and those working full
time but frustrated by the kind of tasks they perform and the pay
they receive. The report looks at the structural imbalances in the
labor force and in the economy, the poor choice of technology in
both industry and agriculture, the underutilization of manpower in
agriculture, the inward-looking orientation of industry, the inappropriate wage and salary structure of labor, and the overexpansion of

20. *Ibid.,* pp. 59-60.
21. International Labour Office, *Matching Employment Opportunities and
Expectations, a Programme of Action for Ceylon* (Geneva, 1971).

the wrong kinds of education. It proposes a rather long, though quite consistent, list of reforms both for the immediate and long-range time periods. In many respects, the report supports measures which are included in the government's development plan but which have not been implemented. As in the Colombia case, the logic of the Ceylon report places highest priority on employment generation and the restructuring of education, labor market, and trade policies to achieve it.

The Colombia and Ceylon exercises, however, are only suggested approaches for achieving employment and income generation in countries faced with unusually serious problems of underutilization of human resources. Their major recommendations have not as yet been incorporated into development plans. The proposed structural reforms are likely to encounter vigorous opposition by entrenched elites, established ministries, and more tradition-bound development economists. The Colombia and Ceylon reports, and others to follow on Iran and Kenya, are only prospectuses; they have as yet not demonstrated a "track record" of accomplishment.

Some countries do appear to have been successful in achieving effective utilization of their human resources. The two most impressive cases are probably Taiwan and South Korea.

During the decade of the sixties both Taiwan and South Korea appeared to have solved, at least temporarily, their problem of mounting unemployment.[22] The growth record of both countries was impressive. For the period 1960-69, Taiwan's annual GDP rate of growth was 9.9 per cent and Korea's was 9.2 per cent as compared with an average of 4.5 per cent in the non-oil-producing developing countries. No other developing country matched this rate. In Taiwan,

22. Much of the background and statistical information for the following section was obtained from Paul Kuznets, "Labour Absorption in Korea Since 1963," Harry T. Oshima and Lai Wen-hui, "Experience of Labour Absorption in Postwar Taiwan," Conference on Manpower Problems in East and Southeast Asia, Singapore 1971; Bela Balassa, "Industrial Policies in Taiwan and Korea," International Bank for Reconstruction and Development, Washington, D.C., August 1970; and Robert d'A. Shaw, *Rethinking Economic Development* (New York: Foreign Policy Association, December 1971).

aggregate reported employment increased at an annual rate of 4.1 per cent during this period and in Korea by 2.8 per cent (where manufacturing employment increased by 11.7 per cent per year from 1963-69). In both countries, the unemployment rate dropped dramatically—in Taiwan from 5.3 to 1.7 per cent between 1963 and 1968 and in Korea from 8.4 to 5.1 per cent. In this same period practically all developing countries were experiencing sharp increases in unemployment, particularly in their urban areas. Taiwan, moreover, had an extremely high rate of population growth, averaging 3.3 per cent for the period 1953-68, the impact of which was reflected in a very high growth of the labor force (2.7 per cent) in the sixties. The per capita gross domestic product in Taiwan rose from $186 in 1960 to $334 in 1969; in Korea it went up from $94 to $221 in the same period. Taken together, the average annual increase in per capita income in Taiwan and Korea was 6.5 per cent compared to a little over 2 per cent in other non-oil-producing developing countries.

Many economists are inclined to attribute these "success stories" to unusual factors. In both cases, there were massive infusions of foreign aid from the United States. In Korea this averaged $172 million (excluding military) per year in the fifties and the first half of the sixties of which $50 million yearly was under P.L.-480 (food aid). In Taiwan, United States aid from 1950 to 1965 averaged $100 million per year (including military). This is about the current level of expenditures of the Nationalist Government on the maintenance of the 600,000-man army.[23] However, according to official statistics, in both countries the ratio of foreign aid to GNP steadily declined—from 8-10 per cent in 1960 to 4-5 per cent in 1964 to below 2 per cent in 1969. Therefore, the importance of this factor is very probably exaggerated. Undoubtedly, foreign aid played some role in the development of these countries, but it was not the critical factor explaining their phenomenal growth.

23. *Conference on Economic Development in Taiwan,* co-sponsored by U.S. Joint Committee on Sino-American Cooperation in the Humanities and Social Sciences and China Council on Sino-American Cooperation in the Humanities and Social Sciences Academia Sinica, Taipei: June 1967.

It is also claimed by many economists that the cases of Taiwan and Korea demonstrate that unemployment and underemployment may be eliminated when rates of economic growth are sufficiently high. If other developing countries could achieve growth rates approaching 10 per cent, so the argument goes, their problems of underutilization of human resources would likely vanish. In short, their argument is that the cause of underutilization of human resources is insufficient economic growth.

A closer examination of the record in both countries, however, leads to quite a different conclusion. It suggests that the high rate of economic growth was the *consequence* of a constellation of policies designed to utilize with maximum effectiveness the country's great wealth of human resources. The critical factors explaining growth of both countries appear to have been:

1. the active promotion of labor-intensive export industries along with discouragement of capital-intensive import-substitution manufacturing;
2. maintenance of appropriate wage and salary levels in the intermediate and modern sectors of the economy;
3. promotion of labor-intensive agricultural development with emphasis on land reform and small-scale farms;
4. existence of relatively well-educated manpower, coupled with provision of opportunities for its effective utilization.

In his paper prepared for the World Bank, Balassa concludes that, following near completion of the process of import substitution in consumer nondurable goods in the late fifties, both Korea and Taiwan initiated an outward-looking development strategy with major emphasis on exports of labor-intensive manufactured goods. This policy was implemented by a variety of incentives and subsidies. The exports contributed to the growth of both countries by effectively utilizing their most abundant resource, manpower, and by economizing on capital. Early in the sixties both countries adopted realistic exchange rates which eliminated the under pricing of capital imports for their modern sectors. The existence of foreign markets for the products of these labor-intensive industries permitted the use of large-scale production methods.[24] The export industries also created demand for domestic materials which further generated income within the country. Many of these export industries were of modest size and, although they underwent substantial technological improvement, they were never highly capital-intensive. This is reflected in the relatively low capital-to-output ratio in Korea and Taiwan as shown in Table I:

Table I
Investment cost of increasing GNP by one dollar, 1960-69

Korea	1.7
Taiwan	2.1
Brazil	2.8
Israel	2.9
Mexico	3.1
Philippines	3.5
Costa Rica	3.8
India	3.9
Chile	4.0
Peru	4.0
Colombia	4.3
Venezuela	4.9
Argentina	5.6

Administrators Review of Development Performance, 1970, Washington, D.C.: U.S. Agency for International Development, Table D.

In Taiwan and Korea manufactured goods accounted for two-thirds and three-fourths of total exports, respectively, while in most other developing countries they amount to less than 5 per cent.[25] In the sixties Korea and Taiwan increased their exports of manufactured goods by 69 and 34 per cent, respectively, in comparison with about 8 per cent for most developing countries. In 1969 the combined

24. In Taiwan, the major manufactured exports were clothing, telecommunications equipment, plywood, cotton fabrics, and plastic articles. It also included food products such as canned mushrooms, pineapple, and asparagus. In Korea, the major manufactured exports were plywood, wigs, clothing, fish products, and cotton and synthetic fabrics. Unlike Taiwan, Korea does not export significant quantities of processed foods, but it does sell raw silk and fresh fish in foreign markets.
25. Balassa, op. cit., p. 10.

exports of manufactured goods from both countries were about three times as large as from Latin America (excluding trade within LAFTA) which has an industrial output eight times larger. It is also important to note that successful manufacturing for export has attracted considerable private foreign investment in both countries.

The rapid expansion of labor-intensive industries in both countries was facilitated to a considerable extent by relatively low wages, which enable them to retain a competitive advantage for their manufactured goods in foreign markets. In 1968, average manufacturing earnings per day were $1.15 in Korea and $1.61 in Taiwan, as compared with $2.50-$3.00 in Singapore and $6.00 in Japan. These wage differentials correspond closely with the differentials in GNP which were: Korea, $159; Taiwan, $242; Singapore, $681; and Japan, $1096. Wages were also low in comparison with many other developing countries at similar levels of GNP. However, they have been rising very rapidly as a result of this economic growth (around 10 per cent a year during the latter half of the sixties) and, as a consequence, both countries are shifting to more sophisticated industries.

In both countries, but particularly in Taiwan, there was extensive land reform and a policy of encouraging small freeholders. In Taiwan, according to Shaw,[26] there is a long history of labor-intensive improvements in the rural infrastructure such as irrigation and access roads, and tremendous resources have gone into extension services, rural credit, marketing, and research. He summarizes Taiwan's success as follows:

Between 1911-15 and 1961-65, total agricultural production quadrupled, despite the fact that population pressure halved the average farm size from about five acres to a mere two and a half acres. All this was done with the intensification of farming using technologies appropriate to the farm size on the island—using irrigation, new varieties, small-scale machinery and diversified patterns of crops (including vegetable, fruits and livestock). During this period the total amount of agricultural work done doubled, as the number of agricultural workers rose 50 percent and the number of days worked by each person increased one-third. The agricul-

26. Robert d'A. Shaw, paper presented to International Manpower Institute, U.S. Department of Labor, Washington, D.C., November 1971.

tural output per worker also rose by 250 percent during this period, so that the productivity and incomes of the growing labor force also increased significantly.

Thus land reform, intensive cultivation without expensive labor-saving machinery, substantial technical and financial assistance, and encouragement of small farms brought about a rural transformation along with the expansion of export-oriented manufacturing industries. And rural development has been further stimulated by decentralization of manufacturing employment. Only about 16 per cent of the labor force in manufacturing is in the capital city, Taipei, the rest being widely scattered throughout the island. This has enabled farm families to work part time in industry. Without any question, therefore, the agricultural sector in Taiwan has provided a rising level of living for an ever-growing number of farm families.

The record of rural development in Korea has not been nearly as impressive. Industry has not been decentralized; rural incomes have not been rising as rapidly; as a result, Seoul has been growing at 7 per cent a year. Thus far the existence of large export markets has been able to counteract this failing. If these markets were to stop growing, these problems might become much more important in the future.

A final explanation for the success of both Korea and Taiwan is the level of development of their human resources. In Taiwan, one factor was undoubtedly the energetic organization-building capacity of the refugees from the mainland who asserted their control over the island. Both countries have had a relatively high generating capacity for medium- and high-level manpower. On the recalculated Harbison-Myers human resources index (which reflects secondary and higher level enrollment ratios), Korea and Taiwan are ranked among semiadvanced and advanced countries.[27] In 1965, for example, Korea had a higher rank than any other Asian country except Japan and Taiwan and compared favorably with all of the Latin American countries except Argentina. On the same index, Taiwan was not far

27. Frederick H. Harbison, Joan Maruhnic, and Jane R. Resnick, *op. cit.,* Appendix VI, pp. 184-85.

below advanced countries such as Norway, Finland, Yugoslavia, West Germany, and Czechoslovakia. Both Korea and Taiwan had high rates of literacy (well over 65 per cent), and both had achieved virtually universal primary education. In 1960, Taiwan had a ratio of 30 engineers and scientists per 10,000 population, which was higher than all other Asian (except Japan), African, and Latin American countries for which data were available, and which was only slightly below France, Italy, the United Kingdom, and Belgium.[28] Clearly, for countries at the low end of the scale on per capita national income, Taiwan and Korea were unusually fortunate in having highly educated labor forces and well-developed educational systems in the sixties. Another important factor, which is not subject to quantitative measures, unfortunately, was a relative abundance of entrepreneurial, managerial, and administrative talent.

The evidence presented above, though incomplete and rather sketchy, lends weight to the conclusion that the high rates of economic growth in Korea and Taiwan in the sixties were attributable to effective mobilization and use of the countries' resources. The most plentiful of these resources was manpower. Economic policies were designed to make the most effective use of manpower in all sectors of their economies. Many of the suggested approaches to solution of the problems of unemployment and underemployment mentioned in this chapter were constituent parts of the "package" of policies included in the development strategies of both countries. External aid, ready access to markets in Japan and the United States, and the already high level of development of human resources were also contributing factors. The two cases provide very strong confirmation, nevertheless, that countries which find the means to develop and effectively utilize their human resources are likely to be those which will have the highest rates of economic growth as a consequence.

28. Frederick H. Harbison and Charles A. Myers, *op. cit.*

3 | Critical Issues in Formal Education

The skills, knowledge, and capacities of people are developed by learning. There are, however, many different ways for people to learn: in school and out of school; on the job and off the job; pre-employment and in-employment; and simply through experiences as participating members of the labor force. In every country there is what may be called loosely "a learning system." For purposes of analysis, we shall stipulate that the learning system has two component parts or subsystems: first, *formal education* and, second, *nonformal education and training.* A definition of each is necessary.

Formal education connotes age-specific, full-time classroom attendance in a linear graded system geared to certificates, diplomas, degrees, or other formal credentials. It is associated mostly with the young. Formal education is thus easily identified; its administration and control in most developing countries is lodged in a ministry of education; its costs are measurable; its outputs are easily identified.

Nonformal education and training, loosely defined as skill and knowledge generation taking place outside the formal schooling system, is a heterogeneous conglomeration of unstandardized and seemingly unrelated activities aimed at a wide variety of goals. Nonformal education is the responsibility of no single ministry; its administration and control are widely diffused throughout the private as well as the public sectors; its costs, inputs, and outputs are very difficult to measure.

Obviously, there is no clear dividing line between formal and nonformal education. Some out-of-school training programs are conducted in classrooms in a formalized fashion. In other cases, persons may work for degrees and certificates without ever attending a school. The distinction is not too important. The main argument is that effective development of human resources requires the integration of both formal and informal processes of education (that is, *learning*) throughout a person's lifetime.

EDUCATION AS AN INDUSTRY

By any standard, formal education is a big industry in any nation; in some developing countries it is the largest. Formal education is one of the greatest consumers of public revenues. It is, in most developing countries, the largest employer of the outputs from secondary schools and institutions of higher education. Education also spawns the demand for more education; the more it grows the more people want of it. Politicians are pressed to promise more of it; parents look upon it as the principal "avenue" of opportunity for their children; international agencies sanctify it as a human right; and economists look upon it as a process of human capital formation. The examination of the "education sector" of any country is thus central to any analysis of economic, social, political, and cultural development.

Formal education performs many functions in developing societies. The first, and perhaps most idealistic, is *enrichment of human life*. Education is supposed to build individual awareness and sensitivity to the world, the community, and humanity. It is considered to be a right of all human beings, even though it is still out of reach of well over half of the people, especially the younger generation, in the Third World countries. Education is also a selection device. As such, it is a powerful force in the formation of a country's elite. Formal education systems are similar to giant sorting machines which determine access to positions of wealth, status, and power. And in performing the selection function, they also simulate barriers which may exclude the "uneducated" from the processes of modernization. Education also *generates values*. It influences the mentality of nations and conditions people's attitudes toward work, co-operation, and relations with neighboring countries. In many cases, education is an *instrument* of *indoctrination* for a creed or political philosophy. Finally, education is one of the *means* for *developing* the *skills, knowledge, and capacities* of persons for participation in the 'labor force. Here education contributes most obviously to human resources development or, in economic terms, to human capital formation.

In the human resources approach, all of these functions are critically important. Although placing major emphasis on skill and knowledge generation and selection of elites, this approach would certainly not deny the importance of enrichment of human life, or any of the other goals of education just cited, as important elements in human resources development.

In performing its functions, however, education can be either a *constructive* or a *destructive* force. It can develop people whose skills are strategic or useless for economic growth; it can help select persons for leadership roles who may promote progress or impose stagnation; it can favor the rich and discriminate against the poor; it can build a work-oriented or leisure-oriented mentality; it can free the mind or strangle it with indoctrination; it can energize people or it can destroy their initiative. Conceivably it could even be irrelevant in shaping today's societies.

Our concern is mainly with the relationships between education and the world of work. The main argument rests on the assumption that, if education can make a positive contribution to the development and utilization of human resources, it is much more likely to perform its other functions constructively. Education, as an industry, is characterized by massive size, rapid growth, escalating demand, and sharply rising costs. No country, advanced or undeveloped, ever seems to have enough education; the need is always greater than the resources available. Everywhere the virtues of education are extolled, while its product is always subject to lively criticism from different sources.

In the United States education employs more manpower than most of the mass production industries. In Nigeria more people are employed in teaching than in all manufacturing and commerce in the modern sector. The typical African country allocates at least one-fifth of government expenditures to formal education, and many spend one-third or more.

Formal education is a very fast-growing industry. Recently, expenditures on education in most countries have been increasing much more rapidly than GNP. In the United States, for example, educational expenditures have risen about three times as fast as GNP during the last two decades. In Nigeria, the annual compound growth rate of expenditure on education in the period 1960-66 averaged about 15 per cent, as compared with an annual growth rate in GNP of about 4 per cent.[1] However, there does not appear to be any fixed relationship between the rise in educational expenditures and increases in GNP per capita. Available data do show rather impressive expansion in student enrollment ratios, although because of rising unit costs, their rates of increase are often much less than those of education expenditures.[2]

In most developing countries, formal education has been easier to expand, at least in quantitative dimensions, than most other sectors of the economy. Consequently, there is a tendency for the proportion of national income devoted to education to rise. The propensity of governments, as well as individuals, to spend ever more resources on education has exceeded the expectations of even its most optimistic advocates. There is little doubt that in all countries, advanced and less developed alike, education has a strong and vocal constituency.

Education is a self-escalating industry. The expansion of primary education generates pressure for expansion of secondary. Increasing numbers of secondary school leavers create a swelling demand for

1. Education and World Affairs, *Nigerian Human Resource Development and Utilization* (New York: Education and World Affairs, 1967), Chap. 9.
2. For some quantitative evidence of recent experience in a number of countries, see Harbison, Maruhnic, and Resnick, *op. cit.,* Chap. VII and Appendix VII. The authors conclude that in nearly all countries during the past ten years expenditures on education have increased more rapidly than GNP per capita. However, they found no fixed relationship between increases in educational expenditures and increases in GNP, suggesting that the forces explaining the emphasis on education may be independent of increases in GNP.

more higher education. And as higher education expands, the pressure for postgraduate studies mounts. As the body of knowledge expands in modern societies, the thirst for learning increases. This thirst seems almost insatiable, so the political pressures for ever greater expenditures for education continue to increase.

In all countries the costs of education tend to rise relative to costs in most other activities. Of all industries, education is one of the most labor-intensive. About 75 per cent of its costs are wages and salaries. In contrast to manufacturing industries which tend to use less labor per unit of output as they modernize, the education industry employs more teachers for a given number of students as it advances. Student-to-teacher ratios are lowered; classes become smaller; special services are increased, for example, counseling and remedial programs; the curriculum is broadened and even perhaps enriched. It is hoped that the quality of instruction is improved as a result. Usually the salaries of teachers rise roughly in parity with salaries of other occupational groups. But, in most other branches of industry, salary and wage increase are offset, at least in part, by corresponding increases in unit outputs as a result of new technology and improvements in management. New technology in education, although it may improve the quality, seldom increases the output of graduates per teacher. If the cost of the very laudable substitution of better trained and more highly paid teachers for those poorly qualified is added, the curve rises even more sharply. Also, as educational systems expand, ever larger proportions of students participate in higher levels of education. The consequences, in terms of unit (or pupil) costs, are discussed later in this chapter.*

Finally, education is, in comparison with other industries, relatively tradition bound. To put it more bluntly, the education industry in most societies is big, basic, and backward. In the advanced countries funds devoted to educational research are only a fraction of those committed to technological innovation in manufacturing, commerce, or transportation. The less developed countries have a propensity to import many of the stagnant and archaic practices of the

* See pp. 70-74.

advanced nations. The growth of education, unfortunately, is too often characterized by "more of the same" rather than imaginative innovation.

In summary, education is subject to an "iron law" of rising costs: on the basis of past evidence, costs rise more rapidly relative to those of production and distribution of other goods and services. At the same time a mounting demand for more education is propelled by irreversible social and political pressures. The proportion of national income allocated to education, however, cannot rise indefinitely. It must level off at some point; otherwise it might consume all of society's resources. Indeed, in the decade of the seventies, education may not be able to attract funds as easily as in the sixties. Government budgetary constraints are likely to become more stringent; external assistance to developing countries may be reduced substantially; indeed, the competition for resources from other industries is almost certain to increase. As a result, planners and educationists will be forced to look more critically at both the functions and the effectiveness of education in relation to the resources which are committed to it.

CRITICAL PROBLEM AREAS

The critical problems connected with the development of formal education systems may be grouped into five categories, which are interrelated:

1. *outputs* of the system;
2. *access* to educational opportunity;
3. *orientation* of the various levels of schooling;
4. *allocation of financial resources;*
5. *organizational and human constraints.*

1. *Outputs*

All countries are committed to the goal of universal primary education. The only question is how rapidly they can achieve it. In the early stages of development, priority may have to be given to secondary and post-secondary education in order to produce critically needed high-level manpower. And indeed the expansion of primary education itself requires training of teachers in secondary-level institutions. In other words, no country can have universal primary education without making substantial investments in the higher levels. What then should be the enrollment ratios at primary, secondary, and higher levels of education, and how are they to be determined?

In some countries expansion of various levels of education is based upon rigorous planning. In Tanzania, for example, the government, in its first development plan, deliberately gave priority to the expansion of secondary education, teacher training, and the university. As President Nyerere reasoned, "Because to plan is to choose, that meant that we had very little money available to devote to expanding the primary school system. And we carried out that decision."[3] By the end of the First Plan, less than 50 per cent of Tanzania's children went to primary school, and in formulating the Second Plan (1969-74), the government announced that universal primary education could not be achieved before 1989. Meanwhile, the president made another hard choice of outputs within the primary education sector. Instead of expanding the number of standard I classes (first grade), the government decided to increase rapidly the number of classes at standards V-VII (grades 5-7) so that every child entering primary school could receive a full seven years of education. In supporting this position, Nyerere argued as follows:

We have made this decision because we believe it is better that money should be spent on providing one child with a 7-year education which may help him or her to become a useful member of society, rather than divide that same amount of money and staff between two children, neither of whom is likely to get any permanent benefit. For the justification of spending money on education in our present economic situation is that this is an investment in our future. Giving a large number of children only four years' education, means merely that we have foregone the present satisfaction of other needs without gaining anything in the future. It is rather

3. United Republic of Tanzania, *Second Five-Year Plan for Economic and Social Development* (Dar es Salaam: Government Printing Office, 1969), Vol. I, p. xi.

as if we spent our money on putting up the walls of two factories knowing that we had insufficient money to put a machine in either, instead of building one factory properly so that it could begin to produce the goods we need.[4]

In other countries, targets may be established in development plans and subsequently upset by unanticipated or uncontrolled pressures. In Nigeria, for example, university enrollments increased from less than 2000 in 1960 to nearly 8000 in 1967, exceeding even the ambitious Ashby Commission goal of 7500 set for 1970. In most middle African countries, the expansion of higher education exceeded the targets in national development plans and, for the area as a whole, the observed increase in enrollment from 1960 to 1965 was 150 per cent, as contrasted with a targeted growth of 91 per cent, at the Addis Ababa and Tananarive conference in 1961 and 1962.[5] In some Latin American countries, the expansion both in numbers of institutions as well as students has been even more impressive. For political and social reasons each major state or region within a country may insist on having a university, whether or not there may be job opportunities for the graduates.

In the sixties Kenya found that it might be impossible to limit the expansion of secondary education. Despite discouragement from the Ministry of Education, large numbers of uncertified "Harambee Schools" sprang up in local communities on the initiative of parents and local authorities. These later had to be incorporated into the formal education system. As a result, the entire system of secondary education was expanded at nearly twice the planned rate, and by 1970 large numbers of secondary school leavers were unable to find places in higher education or jobs in the labor market.

As a general rule, the outputs of the educational system in most developing countries are poorly geared to needs. Of course, no one would argue against providing every child with opportunity for some primary education. But provision of poor primary education, with

4. *Ibid.,* p. xii.
5. UNESCO and OAU, "Regional Education Targets and Achievements," UNESCO-OAU/CESTA Ref. 2 (Paris, 1968).

untrained teachers and without books and appropriate materials, may be a fraud instead of a benefit. In most cases there is a trade off between rapid expansion of very low-quality schooling and slower development of quality education. But, political pressures often force resort to the first expedient. It may be easy to fashion a rational plan for educational development, but there are always formidable obstacles in the way of implementing it.

Once primary education is expanded, the pressures for expansion of secondary and higher levels are increased. Parents will insist that places in secondary schools be available to those completing primary. And universities must expand in response to the clamor from secondary school leavers. And once a country starts to move rapidly along the road of formal education, it must be terribly aware of the precipice of bankruptcy.

The pattern of educational outputs in the typical developing country might be summarized as follows: primary education expands at a relatively slow pace. It is available to most of the children in the urban areas but only to a minority of the rural population. Its quality is usually poor, and dropout rates are high. Primary school leavers for the most part are unable to find employment and thus attempt to enter secondary schools. These are highly concentrated in the urban areas. The "successful" secondary school leavers gain access to universities or other higher education institutions, but most are forced to enter the labor market. Here, modern-sector jobs are scarce, and many graduates remain unemployed or perhaps return to families and relatives in rural areas. Because of pressure from secondary school leavers, universities expand enrollment at a very high rate. But the output of universities far exceeds the availability of good jobs in the modern sectors. Many of the graduates are unemployed or are forced to take jobs for which they feel they are overqualified. The system thus produces "misfits" at all levels. Increasing numbers of young people are unable to find jobs which meet their high aspirations. In the aggregate, there may not be too much education; rather the difficulty is that the outputs at various levels of the system are poorly balanced. The imbalance is partly quantitative, and, as will be discussed later, is partly attributable to inappropriate orientation of schooling at various levels and poor linkages with the world of work. Political and social pressures, however, demand more of the same. Thus, with ever-increasing resources allocated to education, the imbalance is perpetuated if not aggravated.

Ceylon provides a classic example of an educational system which is structurally inconsistent with development needs.

In numbers of pupils and teachers, the growth of Ceylon's formal education system is impressive, and in comparison with most developing countries, there is less inequality of opportunity. But there is a huge surplus of secondary school and university leavers whose education is quite inappropriate for the employment opportunities which are available. As the ILO report stresses among young secondary school leavers aged fifteen to twenty-four with "O" level passes (ordinary level passes on General Certificate of Education examination), the rate of open unemployment is 70 per cent and even higher among women.[6] Yet, the stock of people with some secondary education has been rising at well over 10 per cent per year. If the current trends were to continue, three-fourths of all new entrants into the labor force will have received at least ten years of schooling which has relevance for only a tiny proportion of available new jobs in the white-collar category. There is also a large growing number of university graduates whose expectations exceed any possible level of suitable employment opportunity. In many developing countries, the quantitative expansion of formal education may soon pose the same dilemma: countries which expand their formal education system most rapidly may have the poorest record of generating appropriate skills and knowledge in their labor forces.

2. *Access to educational opportunities*

In countries where education is available to only a few, access is a matter of critical importance. Universal access to primary education is a long way off in most developing countries. In the meantime,

6. See International Labour Office, *Matching Employment Opportunities and Expectations, op. cit.,* Chap. 9.

there is the question of which children will have schooling and which will be denied access to elementary education. The choices are difficult indeed. As mentioned before, in most countries the children in the cities have a much better chance of attending school than those in rural areas. Since in some cases fees are charged, the children of rich parents usually have a decided advantage. These inequities are compounded by the fact that rural schools often have only two or three grades. In Colombia, for example, only 6 per cent of the rural schools are able to offer all five grades of primary education; the majority (over 60 per cent) offer only two. Since functional literacy is seldom achieved in less than three or four grades, much of the education provided in rural areas is virtually worthless.[7] Access to first-level education may also be restricted on the basis of race or tribe. In some of the East African countries, for example, Asian minorities are finding great difficulty in getting their children into schools.

At the secondary level, access is much more restricted; in higher education it is a privilege of only a tiny minority. Enrollment ratios in various levels of education for representative developing countries are shown in Table I.

At the secondary and higher levels, urban dwellers again have a tremendous advantage. In Colombia, for example, the proportion of persons in the rural areas who have had secondary education is smaller than the proportion of persons in the towns who have completed university work. And the number of persons with university education in rural areas is almost insignificant.[8]

The allocation of opportunity for secondary and higher education raises thorny issues. Shall preference be given to those who are best able to pay? To those with the strongest political or tribal connections? To those who are located closest to educational institutions? To those who are considered by some criteria to be best qualified?

Since secondary and higher educational institutions are the principal gateways through which the younger generation must pass to enter the modern sector and to join the ranks of the elites, these are

7. International Labour Office, *Towards Full Employment, op. cit.,* p. 219.
8. *Ibid.,* p. 220.

Table I   School enrollment ratios in selected countries

Less developed countries	1st level	2nd level	3rd level
Afghanistan	17.5	3.3	0.4
Burma	80.2	9.0	1.4
China (Taiwan)	104.6	44.7	14.3
Colombia	93.1	18.3	3.5
Dahomey	35.2	4.9	0.1
Ecuador	95.6	19.2	4.3
Ethiopia	11.9	2.5	0.2
Guatemala	57.8	9.9	2.4
Haiti	42.0	3.9	0.5
India	59.9	34.0	4.2
Jamaica	92.2	23.8	2.4
Kenya	50.9	9.2	0.8
Lebanon	96.5	34.4	14.4
Malawi	34.9	1.8	0.4
Nicaragua	74.6	16.5	3.1
Pakistan	52.3	18.0	3.8
Senegal	44.5	8.7	2.6
Sierra Leone	37.5	7.7	0.4
Sudan	28.5	4.3	0.8
Syria	85.1	38.2	12.2
Tanzania	29.8	1.9	0.1
Thailand	62.5	15.1	2.5
Tunisia	109.9	24.2	2.0
U.A.R.	74.3	28.7	9.5
More advanced countries	1st level	2nd level	3rd level
Argentina	102.3	52.9	17.3
Australia	95.1	74.6	20.2
Belgium	110.7	70.1	16.3
Chile	120.2	34.6	7.3
Czechoslovakia	97.2	40.2	17.1
Finland	117.6	55.0	14.1
France	141.2	54.2	21.2
Germany (West)	111.9	70.1	11.0
Israel	95.8	51.4	24.9

Table I   (continued)

More advanced countries	1st level	2nd level	3rd level
Italy	110.1	44.9	10.0
Japan	95.7	84.6	15.4
Netherlands	104.1	76.9	20.5
Poland	93.2	77.3	16.3
Portugal	84.6	44.9	5.8
Spain	101.4	46.3	6.2
Sweden	99.7	69.5	15.0
U.S.S.R.	101.0	46.8	35.1
U.K.	97.9	99.6	9.4
U.S.A.	115.6	100.5	50.6
Venezuela	87.5	34.2	8.5
Yugoslavia	94.4	44.6	16.4

Enrollment ratios are calculated for *average* duration of schooling at each level and for the relevant age group in the population—first, 5-14; second, 15-19; third, 20-24.

SOURCE: Harbison, Maruhnic, and Resnick, *Quantitative Analyses of Modernization and Development, op. cit.,* Appendix VIII.A.

important considerations. Practices differ by countries and regions. In African countries, entry into the universities depends upon a successful record in secondary school and the passing of examinations. Most of the successful applicants are then supported by government bursaries. In Latin America, the principal screening device may be completion of secondary education, much of which is fee-paying and thus open only to the relatively well-to-do, following which university education may then be free.

Where shall government bursaries be provided? What fields of study (that is, science and engineering as opposed to arts or humanities) will have priority? To what extent can bursaries be used to allocate candidates to those fields of study deemed most important for national development? Here there is often a conflict between the desires of the individual and the needs of the state. Advanced nations may be able to afford the luxury of freedom of choice, but developing countries are more hard pressed to allocate scarce resources to the higher priority needs.

As noted earlier, formal education acts as a sorting machine. To a considerable degree it selects those who may become members of the elites, and it provides the introduction to acquisition of skills and knowledge required in the modern sector. But in its negative sense, it rejects and cripples those who are selected out. What does the future hold for the millions of youngsters, in many countries more than half of the school-age population, who will never have access to any formal education? What will be the effect upon the vast majority of primary school leavers who are unable to attend secondary or higher institutions? These are some of the nightmares which plague the human resources planner. As long as formal education commands the routes to wealth, prestige, and power, it is a system which favors the few at the expense of the many in the developing countries.

3. *Orientation*

The orientation of formal education is a problem in all countries. What is to be taught? What is an appropriate "bias" or emphasis in choice of subjects and fields of study? And what are the stated or implied criteria for success? Unlike outputs and access, orientation can be measured only in qualitative terms, and these stem from value judgments.

The basic bias of most education systems is toward more education. Success at each level is measured by passing tests and gaining entry into the next higher level. Since the university is at the apex of the education system, entry into and completion of higher education are the supreme goals which dominate the entire system. The university thus casts its shadow over every branch and level of education. Those who "make it" through the university have at least the entry passes into prestigious positions in the modern sector, although in many cases more passes are issued than the number of available positions. Those who do not "make it" are, in varying degrees, selected out by the educational screening process as failures. In the developing countries, unfortunately, the possession of formal degrees is much more important as a prerequisite for positions of high pay, status, and power than is the case in the advanced countries.

In Ceylon again, the shortcomings of the orientation of formal education are noted by the ILO report.[9] Instead of pursuing the goal of general education, the secondary schools retain their single-minded concern with qualifying people for white-collar jobs and entry into the university. Dropout rates are extremely high. And the years of study by those who fail the examinations are almost pure waste, because the whole program of the schools is directed toward passing tests. The school's concern with education is thus eclipsed by its commitment to credentialization which is, at best, a dubious indicator of learning relevant to a developing country.

The bias of higher education in favor of arts, humanities, law, and the softer social sciences, in contrast with the hard sciences and engineering, is generally recognized as characteristic of most developing countries. A chorus of criticism contends that the universities produce too few doctors, engineers, scientists, and related technical personnel and turn out too many lawyers and arts and humanities graduates. To the extent that this is true, it probably reflects the inability of secondary school to prepare students adequately in mathematics and science-based subjects. Another reason is that unit costs of university education in the hard sciences are much greater than in nontechnical fields. And finally, it is easier to provide large numbers of students with low-quality education in the nontechnical areas than in medicine, science, and engineering. But the broad criticism of the nontechnical bias needs to be qualified. In an earlier study, we found no significant difference between the proportion of science and technology students in the underdeveloped and partially developed countries as compared with the semiadvanced and advanced nations.[10] In some of the less developed countries the proportion of students studying technical subjects was very high. In India, for example, the universities have been turning out a surplus of engineers.

9. International Labour Office, *Matching Employment Opportunities and Expectations, op. cit.,* Chap. 9 and Summary.
10. Frederick Harbison and Charles A. Myers, *op. cit.,* Chap. 3.

Perhaps a more fundamental criticism of the orientation of higher education is its bias toward the science and culture of advanced countries at the expense of greater concentration on the particular problems of the developing economies. But here relevance to local needs is sometimes indistinguishable from poor quality of teaching personnel, materials, library services, and laboratory facilities. With a few notable exceptions, the quality of higher education in the less developed countries is poor both in comparison with that available in the advanced countries and in relation to local needs.

In nearly all of the less developed countries secondary education has an academic bias. A relatively small proportion of the students attend vocational schools, which presumably prepare young people for direct entry into the labor market; the vast majority are in general or academic schools, which are oriented toward preparation for higher educational institutions. Table II brings out the contrast between relatively advanced and relatively underdeveloped countries. Also shown is the ratio of expenditures per pupil between vocational and general secondary schools. Clearly, the expenditures for vocational schools are many times higher.

An even greater shortcoming may be the orientation of the vocational schools themselves. As a general rule, those which specialize in pre-employment craft training have been failures. They have had great difficulty in placing their graduates, in part because of low-quality instruction which is often not relevant to the specific needs of employers and in part because the graduates, who may have high job aspirations, price themselves out of the market. For the most part, employers prefer to take on youngsters at lower wages and train them on the job rather than hire the outputs of these schools. In many respects, therefore, it may be fortunate that only a very small proportion of secondary-level students are enrolled in vocational schools. They appear to be costly relative to other secondary education and for the most part quite ineffective.

The orientation of primary education is likewise widely criticized. Here again the objective, in addition to developing literacy, is primarily to prepare most students for entry into secondary education.

The vast majority of primary attenders who never make it to secondary are, by the success criteria of the system, failures. The systems of examination are designed to select the few for advancement and to reject the less promising majority. Although ministries may give lip service to primary education as preparation for life, they structure it in practice to filter out only those best suited to advance to higher levels of education.

Table II   Ratios in academic and vocational second-level education

Less developed countries	Number of students enrolled (academic/ vocational)	Recurrent expenditures per pupil (vocational/ academic)
Burma	157.0	5.0
Pakistan	131.5	29.0
Lebanon	56.7	29.6
Guyana	28.7	4.5
Syria	27.7	3.1
Kenya	23.0	1.9
Sudan	20.7	1.5
Dahomey	17.2	4.4
India	16.3	8.6
Sierra Leone	12.9	1.5
Ethiopia	11.1	3.4
Jamaica	10.3	3.0
Malawi	6.5	3.6
Thailand	6.5	2.3
U.A.R.	6.3	2.4
Nicaragua	5.5	2.9
Guatemala	5.3	4.6
Haiti	4.6*	4.6*
China (Taiwan)	4.4	1.6
Colombia	2.8	0.9
Afghanistan	2.4*	2.3*
Tunisia	2.1	0.7
Ecuador	1.7	0.9

Table II   (continued)

	Number of students enrolled (academic/ vocational)	Recurrent expenditures per pupil (vocational/ academic)
More advanced countries		
U.K.	20.5	0.6
Finland	3.9	2.9
France	2.9	1.5
Italy	2.7	1.4
Spain	2.3*	2.2*
Venezuela	2.0	1.3
Chile	1.8	1.3
Israel	1.8**	0.7**
Portugal	1.0	0.7
Netherlands	1.0	0.9
Germany (West)	0.9	0.4
Argentina	0.8**	1.6**
Belgium	0.6	0.7
Yugoslavia	0.4	1.2
Czechoslovakia	0.4*	2.5*
Poland	0.4*	1.3*

* Teacher training included with vocational.
** Teacher training included with academic.
SOURCE: *Unesco Statistical Yearbook 1969* (Paris, 1970), Tables 2.18, 2.19, 2.20.

The developing countries recognize most of the problems and shortcomings mentioned above. Few educational planners will argue in favor of the existing orientation. Most advocate change and reform. And in many cases, the ministries, institutes of education, and university research organizations are working hard on development of new textbooks, methods of instruction, curriculum improvement, and more broadly based testing techniques. Change and reform, however, are difficult within large educational bureaucracies. There are first of all differences among the experts concerning what are the most urgently needed changes; and strategically placed within the hierarchies of formal education are powerful groups of persons, both teachers and administrators, with vested interests in existing ways of doing things. Finally, resources, both human and financial, are usually lacking to mount a sufficiently massive effort for reform. Teachers and administrators in the education industry are likely to favor change only if it does not upset the status quo!

4. *Allocation of financial resources*

Nearly all developing countries are under pressure to increase expenditures on formal education. The reasons are obvious: in most cases the school-age population is rising rapidly; school participation rates are increasing at every level; and, as pointed out earlier, the education industry is subject to an iron law of rising costs. In most countries, expenditures for formal education increase much more rapidly than GNP and, as a consequence, the developing countries continually seem to be spending larger proportions of their income on education.[11]

In many respects the propensity of the developing countries to invest heavily in education is commendable. It indicates awareness of the importance of developing the capacities of people. At the same time, it poses questions. Do rising expenditures result in expansion of educational opportunity to more persons or do they merely reflect higher unit costs? Is formal education always the best way to develop human resources or would greater investment in nonformal training be more effective? And how long can the upward trend in the proportion of resources devoted to education last without jeopardizing the proper allocation of resources to competing activities?

The allocation of resources within the formal education system is also a matter of critical concern. In the developing countries, for example, the per student recurrent expenditures in higher education in comparison with those of primary are usually very high. Table III (column 3) shows this quite clearly. In most of the advanced coun-

11. See footnote 2.

tries, the ratio of per pupil expenditures in higher compared with primary is less than 10 to 1, while the ratios for the developing countries with few exceptions are well above that figure; four of the twenty-four less developed countries (Sierra Leone, Malawi, Kenya, and Tanzania) have ratios ranging from 127 to 283 to 1, and another ten are above 20 to 1. In Malawi, for example, over two hundred students can be supported in primary education for every one at the university level, whereas in countries such as Italy, Japan, Sweden, and the United States, the expenditure for one university student a year is less than three times that for one student in primary. Likewise, in Malawi only a handful of students have access to higher education (about $\frac{2}{10}$ of 1 per cent of all students), whereas in most of the advanced countries, well over 10 per cent of all students may be enrolled at that level. In short, the "sacrifice" made by developing countries to provide university education for a tiny minority may be very great. President Nyerere has expressed this eloquently in his introduction to the country's first Five-Year Plan:

Some of our citizens will have large amounts of money spent on their education, while others have none. Those who receive the privilege therefore have a duty to repay the sacrifices which others have made. They are like the man who has been given all the food available in a starving village in order that he may have strength to bring supplies back from a distant place. If he takes his food and does not bring help to his brothers, he is a traitor. Similarly, if any of the young men and women who are given education by the people of this Republic adopt attitudes of superiority, or fail to use their knowledge to help the development of this country, then they are betraying our Union.[12]

The differences in per cent of students in higher education compared with primary are striking (column 4). In the less developed countries, the ratio of students in primary to students in higher education in all but two cases is above 20 to 1. In half of the countries it is above 100 to 1. Among the more advanced countries, two-thirds have ratios less than 20 to 1; the highest, Chile, is 32; and countries

12. Tanganyika, *Five-Year Plan for Economic and Social Development,* Vol. I: General Analysis (Dar es Salaam: Government Printing Office, 1964), p. xii.

Table III

Less developed countries	Recurrent expenditures per pupil on education (U.S.$)		Ratio (1)/(2)	Ratios between first and third level education	
	1st level	3rd level		Number of students enrolled (1st/3rd)	Recurrent expenditures (3rd/total)
	(1)	(2)	(3)	(4)	(5)
Afghanistan	8	470	1:59	109.3	17.6
Burma	7	141	1:20	83.1	10.4
China (Taiwan)	16	193	1:12	17.7	12.8
Colombia	27	864	1:32	48.1	20.0
Dahomey	38	335	1:9	908.0	0.6
Ecuador	22	343	1:15.5	46.8	14.5
Ethiopia	22	1046	1:47.5	105.5	16.9
Guatemala	33	444	1:13.5	55.1	14.3
Haiti	11	220	1:20	182.2	7.4
India	7	219	1:31	54.9	32.1
Jamaica	34	1882	1:55.5	160.4	3.8
Kenya	22	3133	1:142.5	315.0	13.1
Lebanon	92	309	1:3.5	19.1	6.6
Malawi	20	4152	1:207.5	482.5	14.0
Nicaragua	46	421	1:9	58.2	9.5
Pakistan	6	70	1:11.5	25.2	20.4
Senegal	49	250	1:5	77.6	4.3
Sierra Leone	17	4815	1:283	170.4	43.9
Sudan	60	2702	1:45	52.5	26.0
Syria	27	206	1:7.5	23.8	15.7
Tanzania	22	2688	1:122	958.0	7.4

Tunisia	30	533	1:18	108.3	6.8
U.A.R.	22	224	1:10	20.5	17.0
More advanced countries					
Argentina	72	271	1:4	13.5	16.7
Australia	139	1013	1:7	8.9	27.2
Belgium	163	1808	1:11	25.1	12.7
Chile	48	1046	1:22	32.4	27.4
Czechoslovakia	111	1069	1:9.5	18.0	16.1
Finland	515	1012	1:2	8.6	8.8
France	160	1235	1:7.5	11.9	19.6
Germany (West)	233	1366	1:6	16.2	20.7
Israel	183	824	1:4.5	13.9	20.7
Italy	195	501	1:2.5	15.9	7.4
Japan	151	1295	1:8.5	7.7	12.7
Netherlands	210	2920	1:14	11.5	21.1
Poland	56	779	1:14	21.8	24.1
Portugal	23	131'	1:5.5	23.6	8.9
Spain	42	139	1:3.5	26.3	7.1
Sweden	633	1718	1:2.5	7.0	13.9
U.S.S.R.	310	433	1:1.5	3.7	12.3
U.K.	210	2125	1:10	14.3	23.6
U.S.A.	539	1536	1:3	4.7	28.2
Venezuela	98	1462	1:15	25.1	22.0
Yugoslavia	66	279	1:4	14.2	14.8

SOURCE: *Unesco Statistical Yearbook 1969* (Paris, 1970), Tables 2.18, 2.19, 2.20.

such as Australia, Japan, Sweden, the United States, and the Soviet Union have ratios well below 10 to 1. Clearly, therefore, the developing countries tend to spend large proportions of their education budget on the very small proportion of students who are in higher education.

The pressures for expansion of the higher levels of education in developing countries are very strong, and the same is true of secondary. Unfortunately, these are the levels of education which also are the most costly. Thus in many countries the expansion of higher levels of education may mandate postponement of achievement of universal primary education. And paradoxically, university and secondary school graduates in many cases are finding it ever more difficult to find suitable jobs in the modern sector.

5. *Organizational and human constraints*

It would be a mistake to assume that all, or even the most important, constraints are financial. The formation of human capital, particularly teachers and administrators, also limits the growth and improvement of formal education. In most African countries, the shortage of qualified teachers, particularly in mathematics and science subjects, is a major bottleneck at both the secondary and higher levels. Top quality university teachers are in short supply in almost all branches of higher education. The dearth of competent instructors for vocational schools may be one of the major reasons for their general record of failure. There is widespread recognition of the need for better school principals, as well as for planners, advisers, administrators, and researchers in educational ministries.

It is true, of course, that some countries in Asia and Latin America already have too many school teachers in terms of the effective demand for their services. In other cases, teacher shortages might be quickly alleviated if higher salaries were offered. And personnel can be trained for specialists in ministries given time, effort, and allocation of necessary financial resources. But one must always remember that education, more than most other industries, is highly labor-intensive, and hence its growth and development are particularly dependent on generation of the skill and knowledge of the human resources devoted to it.

The final constraint is the capacity to build effective organizations for the delivery of education. Ministries of education, as well as schools, universities, and other educational institutions are strategic "organizational personalities" in their societies. Some are live and dynamic, responsive to new ideas, and vigorous. Others are tradition bound, resistant to change, and lethargic. Some develop the talents of key personnel in the hierarchy; others stifle initiative and deplete precious human capital. And in all cases much depends upon the men at the top—the organization builders—and their capacity to perceive both the goals of society as well as the artful science of building a team. The less developed countries usually have great difficulty in building effective organizations, in part because of a shortage of organization builders, but probably more because of imitation of organization structures which may be appropriate in the more advanced economics but which are alien to the political and cultural milieu of developing countries. Admittedly, organization-building capacity is not subject to quantitative measurement. But without question, a principal limitation in development of educational services is organizational power failure—the inability to perform effectively the tasks as planned and expected.

COST EFFECTIVENESS OF EDUCATION

The costs of formal education can be determined with reasonable accuracy. Governments usually can calculate both capital and recurrent expenditures for education. The amounts spent by individuals as well as nongovernment institutions may be quantified. Even opportunity costs in the form of foregone earnings may be estimated without too much difficulty. Economists can construct models for expansion of formal education based upon a range of assumptions as to enrollments, inputs of teachers, wastage rates, and other quantitative parameters. The cost implications of choosing one or another path of educational expansion may be ascertained. The costs are likely to be high. The crucial and much more difficult problem is to estimate the benefits of education; here the model builders have much less to offer.

How can effectiveness be compared with costs? And what are the appropriate indicators of the internal efficiency of an educational system? These are the difficult questions which are invariably raised but seldom answered.

Education is supposed to enrich human life by building individual awareness and sensitivity to the world, the community, and humanity. Is this determined by the ability to read, write, calculate, and communicate? Can it be measured by tests, by continuous exercise of such skills, and by growth of an individual's perceptiveness? Many educators rationalize education on these grounds. But they are usually unable to measure progress with hard data.

The generation of skills and knowledge for the labor force is a somewhat more tangible function of education. Effectiveness may be gauged by matching the outputs of the educational system with available or anticipated employment opportunities. Unemployment or underemployment of school or university graduates is an indicator of ineffective gearing of education to national development needs. And it may be relatively easy to show how education can contribute to goals such as self-sufficiency in high-level manpower. At least in part, progress may be measured by periodic manpower surveys.

The evaluation of formal education as a selection device, on the other hand, is a much more uncertain process. Does formal education, with its trappings of requirements, examinations, degrees and certifications, really select those most competent to fill the higher positions in developing countries? Does it favor the children of the rich or those already in the modern sector to the detriment of the poorer masses? And as a screening device, is it fair or arbitrary, consistent or inconsistent with the needs of national development? Understandably, most government officials are reluctant to accept the idea that formal education is a discriminatory mechanism. They are prone to pass over the issue by holding out the promise to provide educational opportunities for all, but in the developing countries such promises are clearly unrealistic. And even when recognizing that formal education is a sorting machine, evaluation is much more likely to be made on the basis of subjective judgments than on the basis of objective measures.

Finally, evaluation of education as a means of building consensus on common goals probably defies any attempt at objective measurement. In Tanzania, for example, education is supposed to stress the values of self-reliance, co-operation, and African socialism, and concerted efforts are being made to orient schooling to this end. Most of the country's leaders and teachers probably espouse this goal. But how can progress toward its achievement be measured other than by personal judgments, impressions, or informed guesses? The "payoff" in building national consensus can be determined only by the subsequent behavior of persons exposed to various kinds of learning experiences.

The measurement of the internal efficiency of education is perhaps a simpler task. One can count the number of dropouts and repeaters at various levels of schooling. In Colombia, for example fewer than 20 per cent of the population have completed five years of schooling, although three to four times as many started primary education. If it takes between three and four years of schooling to make a youngster reasonably literate, it is probable that more than half of those who started school derived little or no benefit.[13] High dropout and wastage rates are characteristic of the educational systems in most developing countries. Obviously, better retention rates in all levels of education would be good indicators of improved efficiency.

The costs of administration can be calculated, and the speed and efficiency of implementation of policy decisions can be ascertained by objective measures. To some extent, the performance of individual teachers may be evaluated without too much difficulty. Thus, the internal efficiency of the education system, which is part of the broader problem of effectiveness, is subject to verification on the basis of relatively tangible criteria.

In recent years, many economists have advocated that effective-

13. International Labour Organization, *Towards Full Employment, op. cit.,* Chap. 15.

ness of education can be based upon cost-benefit analysis which calculates the "rate of return" on investments in education. The estimation of costs on investment poses no serious problem. Benefits are measured by lifetime earnings differentials for various levels of achievement in formal education. This rate of return is discussed more fully in Chapter 7. At best, however, it attempts to measure only one dimension of education—the economic—and even here, the assumption that in the developing countries, earnings reflect the economic contribution of the educated members of the labor force is open to serious question. It is probably safe to say that today few planners and statesmen would place primary reliance on this approach in allocation of resources to formal education, although the calculation of returns may be one interesting exercise, among others, in the determination of effectiveness of education.

An education system must be evaluated from several different perspectives. No single measure, such as the effect on lifetime earnings of individuals or groups, can throw light on more than a tiny part of the problem. The measurement of effectiveness is more often based upon opinions, judgments, and impressions than on quantitative indicators. In the future, as in the past, faith, hope, and politics are likely to dominate the decision-making in educational development.

In the sixties most planners, statesmen, politicians, and international agencies became convinced that formal education was essential for economic growth and nation-building, and thus more of it was without any question a good thing. More sane and sophisticated assessment is likely to emerge in the seventies. In the LDCs there is growing awareness that expansion of formal schooling is not always equatable to the spread of learning, that the preoccupation with certification and degrees is not always consistent with adequate preparation for the world of work, that education which is poorly oriented can distort aspirations, and that overinvestment or unwise investment in formal schooling, particularly at the secondary and higher levels, can be a drag rather than a spur to national development. It will be tragic, indeed, if the development of formal education, together with the vast and the costly machinery of teacher preparation, is based upon more of the same. A linear projection of past trends in educational systems, particularly those inherited from former colonial powers, could be disastrous for the developing countries.

Formal education, however, is only part of a broader system of human resources development. Skill and knowledge generation are not confined to classrooms for the young. Effective learning in a continuous lifetime process. And recurrent education and training are fully as crucial as pre-career preparation. The linkages between formal education and employment are neither direct nor clear; the effectiveness of pre-employment education depends in large measure upon subsequent processes of skill and knowledge generation. In the following chapter we turn to analysis of the system of nonformal education as a factor in human resources development and as a substitute for, as well as an extension of, the formal schooling system.

4 | Nonformal Education and Training

Nonformal education and training encompasses the entire range of learning processes and experiences outside the regular, graded school system. It thus includes everything from learning from parents, communication with others, and learning from experience to formal training on the job, apprenticeship, adult education, and participation in organized out-of-school programs such as youth brigades, extension services, community development projects, and health and family-planning clinics. Probably no country has ever made a complete inventory of all nonformal learning programs conducted by its many public and private agencies; there are no reliable estimates of either capital or recurrent expenditures allocated to them. But in the aggregate, probably more people are exposed to nonformal learning activities than to formal schooling. And as a continuing process of development of skills, knowledge, and capacities of the labor force, nonformal learning and training are certainly as important as formal education.

FUNCTIONS OF NONFORMAL EDUCATION

What then are the actual or possible functions of nonformal education in developing societies?

First, it provides a wide range of learning services which lie beyond the scope of formal education. For example, unskilled and semiskilled workers in factories or in construction must be trained on the job. New skills and knowledge of farmers are best generated through extension and farmer-training centers. And almost by definition, adult literacy programs lie outside of the range of age-specific, graded schooling.

Second, nonformal training and education may be an alternative or substitute for formal education. Here there may be trade offs as far as development policy is concerned. For example, electricians, carpenters, masons, and fitters may be trained in employment either through apprenticeship arrangements or by some less formal means of learning on the job. But they can also be produced under a graded curriculum in formal vocational schools. As a typical case, the training of automobile mechanics illustrates the range of possible choices. In all developing countries there is a shortage of automobile mechanics. Most young people learn the trade as apprentices in small garages and shops as described by Callaway.[1] The indigenous apprenticeship system can be improved by organizing training extension services for the garage owners, as well as by organizing off-duty training classes in the principal towns and cities. The major distributors of automobiles and trucks are better producers of mechanics. They might be required, or encouraged by subsidies, to train a surplus beyond their immediate need in their own service department. Pre-employment formal training in vocational schools is the other, and probably the most expensive, alternative. Combinations of all three avenues of training might in the end provide the most effective solution.

Third, nonformal education is a means of extending skills and knowledge gained in formal education. Human resources development is a continuous, lifetime process. Skills and knowledge generated in pre-career formal schooling may atrophy without the stimulation, extension, and enrichment provided by out-of-school learning activities. For example, technicians are best trained by combining formal instruction in technical institutions with on-the-job experience in the workplace. Civil servants and enterprise managers update their skills through participation in staff training programs. Youth brigades

1. Archibald Callaway, "Nigeria's Indigenous Education: The Apprenticeship System," *ODU*, Vol. 1, No. 1 (July 1964), pp. 67-69.

may be set up to provide more employment-oriented training for school leavers. And agricultural extension workers, suppliers of rural inputs (fertilizers, seeds, tools, and the like), co-operatives managers, and marketing experts need periodic refresher training beyond their formal education. Nonformal education and training, therefore, play an important role in magnifying the benefits of formal education; it is in many cases an indispensible factor in maximizing the returns on initial investment in formal education.

Fourth, nonformal education in many countries may be the only available learning opportunity for large proportions of the population. In many countries universal primary education is a long way off, and most of the adult population may have never attended a formal school. Nonformal education of some kind could fill this gap by providing some minimal learning opportunity for the uneducated masses.

Fifth, nonformal education may be one means of counterbalancing some of the distortion created by formal education. To a considerable extent, formal education establishes the gateways to positions of wealth, status, and power. It issues entry passes in the form of certificates, diplomas, and degrees to a privileged minority; those without the proper credentials are blocked. But competence and learning very often are measured poorly by credentials. Thus, achievement-oriented, nonformal education may provide the means for growing numbers of competent but "uncredentialed" people to gain access to higher level jobs in the economy.

Finally, nonformal education often provides greater opportunity for innovation than centralized formal education bureaucracies do. There is scope for experimentation with new teaching techniques, and new media of instruction and successful innovations may later "spill over" into formal education. Indeed the competition of nonformal programs may force long-needed reforms throughout the formal school structure.

SOME EXAMPLES OF NONFORMAL EDUCATION AND TRAINING

Nonformal education performs important functions, but it has many problems and shortcomings. Some programs are much too costly;

others fail to attract and hold the interest of participants. Most are poorly organized and underfinanced. And the survival of some may depend upon the singular talents of a particular organizer or leader. To understand nonformal education, specific cases must be studied. In this section we look at some examples of nonformal education activities.

1. Learning associated with the work environment

Most nonformal education and training takes place routinely and often unconsciously through learning by doing, instruction or inspiration from others to perform specific tasks, association with peers or fellow workers, or simply participation in a working environment or in the affairs of a community.

A great deal of learning is a response to practical needs. Working environments, as a rule, develop the skills and knowledge which they require. In a primitive subsistence rural economy, simple skills are handed down from father to son. Training is a process of observation and practice. Here, subsistence farmers may be well trained for subsistence farming but not for much else. In modern-sector agriculture, farmers and workers are given specific instruction and supervision (training) in use of fertilizers, insecticides, water use, planting, harvesting, and handling of crops. In this case, learning may be based upon the knowledge of farm managers, extension agents, or extensive research and experimentation. In a modern metal fabrication plant or textile mill, specific on-the-job training is provided for operatives, and nearly all of the craftsmen likewise acquire their skills through in-service training. The automobile mechanics in Nigeria and other African countries learn their trade in small garages or in the larger service shops of the car manufacturers. Only an insignificant few ever learn to become auto mechanics in formal vocational schools. In many of the developing countries the training of personnel to operate complicated oil refineries, chemical plants, and steel mills has been remarkably rapid and effective. Engineers with a professional education learn their specific tasks quickly; operatives, who may have the equivalent of secondary school general education, are trained on the job. And managers and top administrators are in effect "grown" through experience and service during employment. In short, if the education system can produce "trainable people," employing institutions have a remarkable capacity for generating practically all the skills they need.

It is fortunate, indeed, that so much learning takes place more or less automatically without assistance or interference from planners. For example, despite the complaints of managers of manufacturing enterprises that foremen, skilled craftsmen, and competent workmen are in short supply, it is difficult to find cases where production has been seriously impeded thereby. The larger enterprises, particularly subsidiaries or corporations in advanced countries, are usually able to train their own workers, technicians, and clerical personnel by one means or another. Equipment suppliers often provide training assistance to their customers. And in the smaller establishments the owner (a master craftsman) traditionally teaches the trade to his apprentices, who in some cases may even pay for the opportunity of learning on the job. Experience has shown that industrialization may progress without formal vocational or trade schools. The process is, of course, facilitated by the availability of trainable persons with considerable education. Services can be provided by employing institutions. But happily, planners may derive some comfort from the fact that, even if they do very little to train manpower for industrial development, technologically complex working environments have a way of generating most of the skills required if given trainable people with sufficient basic education.

The indigenous training system also works in the rural areas. But here, in contrast to the modern sectors of urban areas where advanced technology has already structured the labor force, the problem is to get the peasants to accept change. Primitive working environments tend to develop only primitive skills, and they employ manpower with little or no education. Modernization demands acceptance of new ideas and new approaches which are often incompatible with traditional skills and knowledge. In order to induce change, it may be necessary to rely on organized programs such as agricultural extension services, farmer training centers, and the spread of general education. However, once the more innovative farmers have successfully adopted a new technology which effectively changes the worker environment, the transmission of know-how throughout the rural community may follow quickly and easily.

2. SENA—A national training scheme in Colombia

Organized programs of nonformal education attract much more attention than routine learning which is inherent in the working environment. The Latin American countries have had notable success in organizing apprenticeship and training programs in close cooperation with employing institutions. SENA* is the largest, most extensive, and best financed training organization in Colombia—probably in all of Latin America. It develops and operates a vast array of training services for workers in commerce, industry, agriculture, animal husbandry, hotel management, and catering, as well as medical services (nurses) and even vocational training in the military.

SENA draws its financial support from a tax of 2 per cent on salaries and wages paid by both public and private enterprises with capital exceeding 50,000 pesos or employing at least ten workers, and from a tax of ½ per cent on salaries and wages paid by the Central Government and the territorial departments and municipalities.

By any measure, SENA is a "big operation" in Colombia. Its total projected expenditures for 1971 were close to 500 million pesos: this was a sum equivalent to about one-eighth of total public expenditures on all education, about a third of expenditures for secondary education, and a little less than half of expenditures for higher education. SENA, moreover, has an assured growth of income based upon payroll taxes.

As a semiautonomous organization within the Ministry of Labor, SENA budgets and controls its own resources, establishes its compensation scales, plans and operates its own programs, and is

---

* This section is based upon a study of SENA by the author in early 1971.

relatively free from control or interference by other government bodies.

SENA provides a wide range of training services in industry, commerce, and agriculture. These include classes in its own training centers (over one hundred), training within enterprises, mobile training units in both rural and urban areas, and consulting assistance to enterprises.

According to the Plan for 1971, SENA had a total of 337,000 persons in all training programs. The grand total of trainee hours is estimated at 68,391,500. Thus the average class time in training per student was about 200 hours. A breakdown by major categories is shown in Table I.

Table I

Formal apprenticeship training (three-year program)	Number of students	Trainee hours
Agriculture, etc.	8,324	8,579,712
Commerce	9,539	9,903,784
Industry	11,398	10,215,920
TOTAL	29,261	28,699,416
Training of adults		
Agriculture, etc.	20,848	3,725,028
Commerce	74,501	9,859,745
Industry	59,044	9,464,947
P.P.P. Rural	87,795	8,896,082
P.P.P. Urban	65,818	7,746,282
TOTAL	308,001	39,692,084
GRAND TOTAL	337,262	68,391,500

Formal apprenticeship training thus involved about 9 per cent of the trainees but nearly 42 per cent of training hours, whereas the P.P.P. (rural and urban basic training, largely for the unemployed and underemployed) accounted for nearly 45 per cent of trainees but only about 22 per cent of total training hours.

Within these broad categories there is a very wide range of training programs, from foreman and supervisory training to short courses for semiskilled industrial, agricultural, and commercial workers. In 1971 SENA planned to operate more than 1000 classes. Consulting and technical assistance was given to about 1200 enterprises. This is a rapidly expanding activity. In 1969 it involved only 250 enterprises; by 1974 it is expected to reach 2200.

Excluding the P.P.P. programs for the unemployed which have been initiated only during the last year, many of the SENA trainees are employed in public or private enterprises, but most of the actual training, probably more than 80 per cent, takes place off the job in the SENA training centers.

SENA develops its programs in response to requests by enterprises and government agencies. It also is guided by regional manpower surveys which it undertakes itself. Its training programs are thus constantly changing. Some of the more significant new programs are vocational training in the military and the mobile units which provide basic training in simple skills for those seeking employment in the modern sector. In general, the entire SENA operation is geared to the needs of the modern sector. In effect, SENA is the servant of its constituency, the enterprises—both public and private—whose payrolls are taxed to support its activities.

However, SENA has many problems. One criticism is that it has trained some persons for whom there were no jobs. Another is that it has failed to provide training where shortages exist. There is evidence that some SENA-trained workers are unable to find employment. And some employers complain that the quality of training is poor in some areas. For the most part, however, employers, unions, and workers are reasonably well satisfied with the relevance as well as the quality of the training. SENA maintains very close contacts with industry; it is under obligation to provide training to meet the specific needs of employers; it employs competent teachers and pays them well; and its human resources division makes continuous assessments of manpower requirements. But it does need a better system for evaluating the effectiveness of its various training programs. The experience of persons completing courses is seldom traced, and the payoffs of training in terms of increased wages and salaries are not measured. The human resources division, however, has made some "opinion surveys" of course completers, but these provide little hard data. Perhaps the most crucial area for follow-up evaluation is the impact of the newly initiated rural and urban basic skill development programs for the unemployed.

SENA has been criticized also for the very high cost of many of its training programs. For example, the unit costs for apprenticeship training probably exceed those for many categories of university students. Even the shorter courses for semiskilled workers have higher per student costs (in terms of instruction hours) than in many kinds of secondary education. The high costs of training may be the result of several factors: rapid expansion of the whole program, the necessity to provide a very large number of specialized courses to meet specific training requirements, the quality of training provided, the relatively high salaries paid to instructors, the high cost of plant and equipment in very modern and elaborate training centers, and rather high costs for instructional materials and administration. Another basic reason for high costs may be the easy availability of financial resources provided by the tax on payrolls.

SENA is thus a massive, far-reaching, organized system of training which is separate from the formal system of education. In some respects the two systems are complementary, but there is also much duplication and overlapping of their activities. For example, the vocational schools, the new multipurpose secondary schools (INEM schools), and the projected junior colleges or polytechnic institutions (all under the jurisdiction of the Ministry of Education) are involved in the development of the same kinds of skills which SENA develops. Presumably, SENA concentrates on training employed manpower, whereas the formal education system is primarily concerned with preemployment education and training, but the lines of demarcation are not at all clear.

Many of the established ministries, particularly education, would like to tap SENA's financial resources to help finance some of the activities of the junior colleges and the multilateral secondary schools. Some have suggested that SENA funds should be used for training outside of the modern sector. Up to now, however, SENA has resisted all attempts to share its payroll tax income with other organizations. It has mantained its exclusive prerogative to manage and spend all of its own resources.

The great danger is that the new secondary schools and polytechnics may duplicate the facilities, machinery, and even teaching personnel of SENA. There is much talk about joint use of facilities and teaching personnel as well as co-ordination of activities, but concrete programs for effective integration at the local level are at best only in the initial stage of development.

SENA-type programs are in operation in most Latin American countries. They are under consideration in many Asian countries, and legislation for establishing payroll tax-supported training and apprenticeship programs is being introduced in a number of the African nations. The idea is being pushed actively by the ILO. Ministries of education, however, are likely to oppose introduction of such schemes because they encroach upon traditional jurisdictions and may lead, as in Colombia, to establishment of dual systems of training. But, on the whole, these programs have many attractive features for developing countries. The payroll tax is an effective means of raising large sums of money without putting strain on the budgets of ministries of education. The semiautonomous organizational structure allows for participation by employers and trade unions in programming free from the encrustrations of traditional ministries. And the emphasis on on-the-job or close-to-the-job training results in more relevant skill generation. But there may be shortcomings also. The funds raised through payroll taxes may be diverted to non-training or even political purposes. Unit costs in many cases may be very high, as in the SENA experience. And powerful and well-headed organizations, even though they are independent of established government ministries, can accumulate bureaucratic encrustations of their own which could destroy their capacity to innovate.

3. *Village Polytechnics*

Unlike the well-established SENA-type national training schemes, the village polytechnics are locally sponsored, relatively new, and still in the experimental stage. They are rurally based. The description given below is based on a study by John Anderson of their operation in Kenya.[2] Quoting from his summary, the concept of the village polytechnic is as follows:

The aim of the polytechnic movement is education for self employment. This means providing young people with skills, understanding and values which will lead them, even when permanent wage earning roles cannot be found for them, to look for other worthwhile occupations in the rural areas. Whilst this aim is laudable, it must be recognized from the outset that no matter how well conceived and run, polytechnics can only play a part in this process which will require carefully planned and coordinated development in many fields including those of agriculture, marketing and rural industry. As educational institutions, polytechnics can present the necessary ideas and skills and at best they can help their students to develop a fuller understanding of their environment in which new worthwhile occupational opportunities can be recognized; improved methods of keeping bees and the making of smokeless cookers are cases in point. But polytechnics cannot, by themselves, do much to create such opportunities.

The key to the evaluation of polytechnics then lies in their capacity to create a new understanding of the opportunities in the rural areas for their students, and their ability to build upon this by providing sufficient training to exploit such opportunities, rather than the ability merely to provide skill training for wage employment as it is currently recognized.

Inevitably the early efforts of the polytechnics focused on skill training, and skill training as such is still their major activity to the extent that in certain polytechnic catchment areas the over production of common skills —carpentry, leather work, etc.—is a clear danger. However, the experiences they have gained in running polytechnics have alerted most of the organizers and staff to this situation and as a result they are now experimenting both to find new occupations in rural life and to help develop the necessary knowledge and skill to help their students take advantage of

2. John Anderson, "The Village Polytechnic Movement" (Nairobi: Institute for Development Studies, University of Nairobi), IDS/SRDP Research and Evaluation Unit. Evaluation Report No. 1, August 1970 (mimeographed).

them. One key factor already brought to light by polytechnics is the multiple nature of occupational roles in rural Kenya where men are likely to be farmers and traders, as well as contracting artisans, if they have the skills.

Thus, in nearly every case polytechnics are developing courses which add elements of commercial training and agriculture to basic skill training. Besides this, in some cases, interesting schemes are being tried which aim to provide help for young people with occupations they find for themselves at their own homes. Such schemes are interesting and show the type of potential which imaginative and flexibility developed rural educational institutions might have. But it must be remembered that such experiments as yet are few and far between, rely heavily on the leadership and initiative of exceptional people who usually, through their church connections, give much of their time voluntarily, and also depend on considerable institutional and financial support from the national church and voluntary aid agencies. There is a clear need for special government aid beyond the current general self help support given by the Department of Community Development. Initially this aid should be aimed at keeping the present experiments going and enabling selected new experiments to be developed. Only when the potential which the polytechnics seem to offer has been explored fully can the Government expect to extend polytechnics development, and even then the extension must evolve following a carefully worked out plan in which local initiative is used and respected. Further, any long term plans for the development of polytechnics must be integrated effectively into an inter-ministerial overall plan for speeding up rural development and increasing employment opportunities.

The concept of the village polytechnic is sound. The development of skills in rural areas which are not completely oriented to urban, modern-sector employment can contribute a great deal to rural development. But the polytechnics have their shortcomings too. In some cases the students consider their training as a first step for getting jobs in the urban areas, thus encouraging rural-urban migration. Other difficulties are the shortage of competent leadership and instructors at the local level, as well as financial support for their services. A final problem is the unavailability of opportunities in many rural areas for the ex-students to make a living practicing their trade. At present the village polytechnic movement is more of an idea than a practical reality, but as such it certainly deserves serious attention and study of its potential usefulness as a means of implementing rural development.

4. *Multipurpose rural training centers*

Another potentially important nonformal education activity is the integrated multipurpose training center. A plan for development of rural adult education centers in Kenya is a good example.*

Here the Board of Adult Education, in collaboration with the Ministries of Cooperatives, Social Services, Agriculture, Health, Commerce and Industry, Information and Broadcasting, Local Government, and Economic Planning and Development, has evolved a concrete blueprint for multipurpose training centers at the district level which will provide facilities to both government and voluntary agencies to plan, integrate, and implement a number of related adult education activities ranging from agricultural extension and simple crafts to literacy and health services. The centers, each with a resident director and staff, will determine priorities, co-ordinate rural educational activities at the district and subdistrict levels, and facilitate the execution of programs. They would provide for maximum involvement of the local community in building programs directly related to the Special Rural Development Projects which are being established as an outgrowth of the Kericho Conference. They would thus constitute the apex of all rural extension and nonformal educational activity. This plan, essentially an extension of the farmer-training center concept, raises many practical problems of inter-agency co-operation. But at least it is an attempt to rationalize the delivery of much needed rural services.

At least at the planning stage, the multipurpose training center idea is taking hold in many developing countries. In some cases, as in Tanzania, the village school may be the nucleus. As contemplated in the Second Development Plan, "The school will . . . become a community education center, at which the provision of primary edu-

---

* The information for this section was gathered from unpublished materials of the Board of Adult Education in Kenya.

cation is only one function, and . . . so conceived will increasingly become a focal point for total educational needs of the community, rather than serving as a somewhat detached institution for the education of children."[3] There is a similar plan for development of rural education centers in Colombia. Such centers would consist of a primary school teacher (or teachers), an agricultural extension group serving farmers but tied into the school, an adult education teacher (or teachers) responsible for functional literacy of adults, a health extension service, and possibly vocational training specialists from SENA.

The merging of many separate nonformal education activities into rural learning centers has great potential. But implementation of the idea faces many obstacles. Ministries and voluntary agencies have vested interests in their particular programs—whether they have extension services, farmer-training centers, literacy programs, health services, sewing classes, or primary education. An integrated center cuts across lines of authority from national ministries to local areas. It must have a head or principal to co-ordinate programs at the local level. And above all, there must be direct communication and lines of authority from the principal to higher levels of government which are in positions to allocate funds and personnel to the centers. An integrated rural training center is usually the responsibility of no single ministry. Because of interagency competition or sheer inertia, multipurpose training centers are still more in the "paper stage" than in actual operation.

5. Mobile training units

Mobile training units are another organized nonformal activity with great promise. The Mobile Trade Training School Program in Thailand is a case in point.*

In 1970 there were thirty-six mobile schools. Each had a principal

---

3. United Republic of Tanzania, *Second Five-Year Development Plan, op. cit.,* p. 157.

* Information based upon unpublished material supplied by the Ministry of Education in Thailand.

and staff capable of training four to five hundred students in a term lasting about five months. At the end of each term, the school is packed up and moved to a different location, usually in rural areas. Training is offered in auto mechanics, radio repair, electricity, welding, tailoring, barbering, hairdressing, food preparation, dressmaking, typing, and bookkeeping. The trainees must be at least fifteen years old, be able to read and write, and pay a small fee. The duration of training in each speciality is about 300 hours, or 3 hours per day for 100 days. As a general rule, those completing training are not highly skilled craftsmen, but they do acquire the knowledge and hand skills to work under the supervision of a skilled worker.

The Mobile Trade Training School Program is apparently very popular in Thailand; in 1968 it provided training to 20,000 people and is expected to reach 60,000 when it becomes fully operational by the mid-seventies. Although discussed here as a nonformal training program, The Mobile Training Schools come under the jurisdiction of the Ministry of Education and are considered as alternatives in rural areas to formal vocational trade schools.

SENA, in Colombia, also makes extensive use of mobile training units both in rural and urban areas. For urban areas and the larger towns in the country, equipment is transported in large vans or trucks. But in the more remote rural areas, both equipment and staff must be transported by donkeys.

As in the case of so many other nonformal training programs, there have been almost no systematic studies of cost effectiveness of mobile training units. Some persons in SENA claim that costs are considerably lower than in the larger urban training centers. Many, of course, claim that the effectiveness of training is much greater compared to formal vocational schools. Certainly mobile units can increase greatly the access of rural dwellers to productive training services. On the other hand, a possible drawback is that both the Thailand and SENA projects are of limited value to persons who are already literate. Certainly, the idea of itinerant training units could be extended to fundamental education and literacy as well as health and family-planning programs.

6. *Mass education by television*

A final example of nonformal training is the use of television in an organized setting.* Here again we describe a program in the experimental rather than a fully operational stage, the case being *Capacitacion Popular* in Colombia.

Capacitacion Popular is an innovative and potentially far-reaching scheme for generating literacy among the disadvantaged urban masses. In Colombia a very large proportion of the urban dwellers are illiterate, and the aim of the government in pushing the program is to provide a way for the under-class masses to participate in the modernization process.

In the developed countries, educational television is used to supplement the tasks of the teacher and thus to improve education in formal schools. The concept of *Capacitacion Popular,* in contrast, is to provide a *substitute* for teachers. The idea is to use volunteer tele-teachers as "guides" or intermediaries between pupils and television programs received in *telecenters*. Instead of building schools, *telecenters* are set up in community action headquarters, co-operatives, churches, or social centers.

The operation is as follows: a monitor, not a conventional teacher, acts as pedagogical intermediary between the pupils and the television set. He is a volunteer from the community, who guides the activities of the learners in the telecenter and in the community and who renders his services free for one hour a day.

The guides may be civil leaders, high school graduates (*bachilleres*), university students, or educators willing to render a social or civic service to the community. It is necessary that these leaders know how to read and write correctly, understand elementary mathematics, have a minimum capacity for guiding and organizing groups, and are service minded. The monitor must attend a basic course which is organized and operated under the direction of a specialized department within *Capacitacion Popular*. In addition, the guides receive systematic instruction after the basic course.

* Information based upon personal interviews by the author.

Two types of efforts are required from the adult participants: an *individual* and a *collective* one. In the former, people must pay one peso for each text (there are eight such texts for the basic literacy component of the program, five for the arithmetic component). The community effort consists of the people collecting the necessary funds to buy the television receiver, which is provided at low cost under a government subsidy. It is expected that these telecenters will become focal points of adult social and community action.

In 1971, only the basic education course was being broadcast. This course, consisting of televised programs and work books, covered five areas: (1) functional literacy, (2) elementary arithmetic, (3) civics, (4) health, and (5) religion. The course was broadcast daily from Monday to Friday for a total of 150 hours. Within each hour of broadcast, lessons corresponding to the five subjects were given.

In 1971, *Capacitacion Popular* was still in the experimental stage. The goal for the year was to reach about 20,000 adults, and this was an optimistic estimate. The televised programs themselves were described by some observers as traditional, dull, and unimaginative. The recruitment, selection, and training of the volunteer monitors or guides also posed serious questions. It was uncertain whether monitors could be recruited on a volunteer basis or whether some form of monetary compensation would be necessary. Apparently, many monitors got bored with teaching the basic course and after a year or so had to be shifted into work related to promotion of the program in the slum communities. The political orientation of the monitors was another problem. The government did not rule out those with anti-government attitudes but preferred persons sympathetic to the goals of the coalition.

The most encouraging feature of the program is the recognition of the need for systematic evaluation of its impact on the target groups. Some of the proposed research questions are: What is the social and economic status of the target group? To what extent do the programs relate to such status? Are the symbols, texts, etc., relevant to problems, levels of understanding, and extent of social and political awareness of the target groups? What impact does the program have on attitudes, understanding, and literacy of the target groups? Does it really serve to involve these groups in the social and political processes of national development?

Even the initial experience with this program suggests that the technical problems of broadcasting and providing television receivers are easily solved. It is much more difficult, however, to design teaching materials which communicate effectively with the participants. It may take many years of experimentation and research to produce the appropriate "software" for illiterate adult groups. Until this can be achieved, the main difficulty with this activity, as with most other attempts to use mass media to promote literacy, will be to hold the interest of participants.

Many more cases of nonformal education could be described. There are work-oriented adult literacy programs which utilize as basic vocabularies the words most commonly used in agricultural and industrial activities. There are programs which offer simple technical and managerial training to small-scale entrepreneurs. In every country there are thousands of private training-for-profit enterprises which teach typewriting, bookkeeping, and specific crafts. Churches offer practical courses in nutrition, agriculture, and home economics; and political parties provide workshops in social, political, and community development. Nonformal education and training activities are ubiquitous and self-generating; they are the work of imaginative and energetic people. Every country has some successful projects, and all have their share of failures. As yet, however, neither statesmen nor planners have been able to evaluate the contributions of this motley assortment of activities to national development.[4]

SUMMARY AND CONCLUSION

The range of activities in nonformal education is vast. The resources already invested in them are very considerable in the aggregate. Their

4. In a recently published survey, however, the African-American Institute has made a substantial contribution in describing and evaluating a large number of nonformal education programs in Africa. See James R. Sheffield and Victor P. Diejomaoh, *Non-Formal Education in African Development* (New York: African-American Institute, 1972).

contribution to national development is far-reaching. In some cases, nonformal education is the only practical means of skill and knowledge development; in others, it offers an alternative to education and training, often a more effective one than formal schooling; in many cases, it supplements, extends, and improves the processes of formal education. Nonformal education provides a fertile field for innovation in learning processes, and in some cases it offers an additional route by which energetic and imaginative people may gain entry into positions of high status and leadership.

In theory it would be desirable for every country to make a complete inventory of all nonformal education, to evaluate the usefulness of each separate activity, to plan extension and improvement of the most promising programs, and above all to build a strategy for their integration into a more logically consistent and better functioning system. The formulation of such a strategy, however, is no easy task. The activities are many and diverse, and responsibility for their operation is highly decentralized. The best procedure is probably to concentrate on a relatively small number of "leverage points" or programs where concentrated effort might have the highest payoffs. For such an analysis, these may be the critical questions:

1. In what important areas can nonformal programs fulfill education and training needs which formal schooling is unable to provide?
2. Are nonformal programs, because of their flexibility in comparison with the rigidities of formal education, more susceptible to innovation in the learning process?
3. In what ways do innovations in nonformal education and training induce desirable innovations in the formal schooling system?
4. In what areas do nonformal activities provide more effective learning, or learning at lower costs, than alternative programs in the formal education system?
5. To what extent can concentration on nonformal programs remedy the defects of limited access to learning provided by the formal system?

These questions suggest, however, that nonformal education and training can be appraised best by examining their relationship to formal schooling. There is no precise dividing line between the formal and nonformal education systems. Rather the activities of both are ranged along a continuum of learning processes.

5 | The Problem of the Balance of Brains

The developing countries are both importers and exporters of persons with critical skills and knowledge. In this chapter we refer to them as high-talent manpower which is strategic for development. Their numbers and occupations may vary widely from country to country, but in general they include scientists, engineers, agronomists, physicians, higher level teachers, experienced managers, journalists, entrepreneurs, and organization builders. In aggregate terms, such high-talent manpower is only a tiny fraction of the labor force, but its role in national development is crucial. This group is the nucleus of a country's brainpower. Some of its members are developed inside the country; others may be brought in from abroad. Unfortunately, many migrate to the advanced nations. The developing countries thus may have both a "brain gain" (through producing and importing high-talent manpower) and a "brain drain" (through out-migration of such manpower). Like the balance of trade, the balance of brains may be an important strategic factor in national development.

There are many ways of importing high-talent manpower. It may be forced upon a country as in the case of colonial administrators in Africa or Asia. It is brought in by large foreign enterprises engaged in commerce, manufacturing, mining, banking, or other activities. The developing countries may actually "rent" high-talent manpower by employing foreigners for fixed periods of time. And possibly the most prevalent means of importing talent is through technical assistance from multilateral agencies or individual countries. The loss or export of talent takes place when highly educated persons outmigrate in response to higher pay and better employment opportunities abroad or when they are forced out of the country by political or social forces. Characteristically, the market for high-talent manpower is worldwide, and for this reason it is difficult for developing countries to control the outmigration of some of their most highly educated persons. But to some extent, gains and losses of strategic manpower are a consequence of deliberate policy choices in national development strategy.

PROBLEMS OF IMPORTING TALENT

A major objective of all Third World countries is to become self-sufficient in high-talent manpower. No country wants to depend indefinitely upon foreigners for performance of strategic social, political, and economic functions; it must always reserve its best and most prestigious positions for its own nationals. Thus, most developing countries properly look upon imported brainpower as a temporary, expendable resource.

Most countries import talent to perform tasks which local nationals cannot undertake. In many African countries, expatriates are still retained in top technical and administrative posts in government. Manufacturing enterprises require foreign managers, engineers, and supervisors at least in the early stages of operation. Technicians are needed to show local nationals how to install and operate complicated equipment and machinery imported from the advanced countries. Experienced foreign scientists are usually required to plan and direct research in agriculture, forestry, or fishing. In particular, universities will call upon foreign scholars for teaching and research in many different areas of knowledge. Perhaps the most common kinds of imported talent are consultants and advisers for planning everything from village water supplies to education systems and regional or national economic development.

There is no dearth of supply of outside brainpower, but the developing countries often pay a high price to obtain it. Multilateral agencies, such as UNESCO, ILO, and FAO, are usually more than anxious to provide experts. In fact, they are prone to flood the developing countries with survey teams and appraisal missions. The World Bank dispatches an endless stream of consultants to assist in the identification and justification of projects for loans. Private individuals and foundations are continually looking for opportunities to invest in pilot projects with a "high-multiplier" effect. In some cases the unsuspecting developing country simply does not have enough local personnel to talk with these external experts, let alone to take their advice. In short, many developing countries may experience a kind of "consultant indigestion" which in its more acute form can virtually paralyze the development process. The planning, ordering, and coordination of technical assistance is thus a high-priority requirement but one which many developing countries find difficult to manage.

Another pitfall is reliance on outsiders to perform tasks rather than to develop people. As an expendable resource, the most important use of expatriate experts is as "seed corn," to build the skills, knowledge, and capacities of local manpower. Their principal function should be that of educators and trainers. But frequently, expatriates cultivate the art of making themselves indispensable in performing particular tasks. The fault is not always theirs. The inability of the developing country to provide counterparts to be trained is a common complaint. In addition, counterparts once trained may be siphoned off to quite unrelated activities.

A third problem is the quality of imported brainpower. Experts from an advanced country frequently lack the required skills for operating in a developing country. Narrow technical training in an industrialized world may be a disadvantage rather than an asset for activities in rural development or small industry promotion. The expatriate university professor, who concentrates on research geared to his advancement in the home country instead of to the practical needs of developing societies, is a poor resource. Perhaps worst of all are the "experts" of mediocre talent who cannot find jobs in the advanced countries and thus depend upon employment in a developing country for a full-time career. It is very difficult to select the best qualified people especially if they are being "rented" for only a brief period. It is even harder to control the selection of consultants and experts sent by the donors of technical assistance.

The availability of outside brainpower is thus a mixed blessing. In one sense the developing countries cannot live without imported brainpower; in another, they encounter great difficulty in living with it. In searching for the solution to the dilemma, a developing country is faced with the following questions:

1. In what period of time can the country become self-sufficient in high-talent manpower, and what are the priorities, in terms of occupational categories, for replacement of expatriates by local nationals?

2. What is the country's capacity to digest technical assistance from abroad and, in terms of national objectives, what are the priorities for such assistance?

3. How are counterparts—or potential replacements for imported manpower—to be selected, allocated, and committed for training, and how can their progress and performance be evaluated?

4. What pressures and incentives can be used to induce foreign-owned enterprises to play a more vital role as generators of skills rather than simply as producers of goods and services?

5. Where shall responsibility be placed for co-ordination of the import of talent so that it can make its most effective contribution to the generation of skills and knowledge of highest priority to the nation?

THE LOSS OF BRAINPOWER TO ADVANCED COUNTRIES

Paradoxically, the underdeveloped countries which have the most acute shortages of high-talent manpower are usually the ones which make the least effective use of it. They often lose the brainpower which they need the most, not because they are unable to develop it, but rather because of their inability to utilize it fully. Some of the developing nations produce many more university graduates than they need; a few turn out even engineers and scientists for whom there are no jobs in the home country. It is ironic, indeed, that countries with the most critical shortages of high-talent manpower often are those with a surplus of highly, but inappropriately, educated people.

The loss because of the investment in training of high-talent manpower may be considerable. In many African countries, for example, the cost of supporting a student for a year in the university is close to $3000, a figure which may be as high as thirty to thirty-five times the average national per capita income. The cost is lower in Asian and Latin American countries, but it is still relatively high in comparison with that in the advanced countries. Much more serious is the loss of the very best and most talented individuals. They are invariably the ones who have the greatest opportunity to migrate to greener pastures abroad. This group rarely exceeds 10 per cent of all highly educated persons, but it is vital to the modernization process. It constitutes the bridge to the developed world; it plans, inspires, and manages productive activity; it spearheads the structural and institutional changes required for development. This top fraction of a country's labor force—the elite of brains—dominates the building of the working environment for most of the labor force. It is the principal source of replacements for expendable expatriate manpower. A developing country needs a critical minimum mass of talent of this kind, and in many cases even the loss of a handful of individuals can be disastrous.

High-talent manpower may leave the developing countries for many reasons. First, earnings possibilities are much higher in the advanced countries. The competition for most high-talent manpower is keen. A well-educated person has credentials for employment in an international market. High earnings, moreover, are not the only, nor even the most important, factor. Many members of the talent elite migrate because there are no established jobs for them at home, because they see no future as professionals, because they have little opportunity to utilize their skills, because they are unsympathetic with the aims and operations of their governments. Employment abroad offers more opportunities to be creative, to work with respected professional colleagues, and to be held in esteem, in contrast to conformity to the rigidity of local government employment, the power of entrenched professors, the deadening inertia of traditional institutions, the dearth of funds for research, professional isolation, inability to move from one career ladder to another, and possible prejudice based upon race, national origin, tribe, or caste. As members of an international talent elite, therefore, those who migrate are "pulled" by more promising opportunities in the advanced world and also "pushed" by inadequate employment, lack of recognition, and traditional obstacles at home.

What then are the roots of the problem? Where must the developing countries look to find the avenues for solution? These questions are thoroughly explored in a definitive study of international migration of talent by Charles Kidd and a number of associates,[1] whose major findings may be summarized briefly.

A major cause of the brain drain is the distorted growth of higher education. In most developing countries during the past decade there has been an unexpected oversupply of university graduates in relation to existing and even anticipated demand for their skills. In some, such as India, even doctors, scientists, and engineers have become surplus, not with respect to human needs, but in relation to effective demand for their services. It is clear that some of the Third World countries can turn out university graduates much more rapidly than their capacity to employ them. The result is unemployment, underemployment, and migration of brains from the country. In reality, therefore, the situation in many countries may be an overflow rather than a drain of highly educated persons.

The distortion in the higher education system is qualitative as well

---

1. Committee on International Migration of Talent (of Education and World Affairs, Inc.), *The International Migration of High-Level Manpower* (New York: Praeger, 1970). Members of the committee were Charles V. Kidd (chairman), George B. Baldwin, Robert Clark, Frederick H. Harbison, John L. Thurston, and Dael Wolfle. This work includes case studies of Taiwan, the Philippines, Japan, Thailand, Korea, Malaysia/Singapore, India, Turkey, Iran, Tanzania, and Kenya as well as general analyses of the Asian subcontinent, East and Southeast Asia, the Middle East, Africa, Latin America, and Europe. Part VIII—Conclusions—presents a summary analysis.

as quantitative. The universities may turn out too many lawyers and arts graduates and not enough technical personnel. Or, as is more often the case, they produce the wrong kinds of technical skills. Scientists, for example, will not be content for long if their principal employment is in secondary school teaching. Engineers cannot be expected to be happy in minor technical or administrative positions in government. A research scientist or engineer must have challenging tasks to perform and access to appropriate laboratories. The commitment of resources in higher education to training high-level technical specialists without advance preparation for maximum utilization of their skills is tantamount to investing in jet aircraft before building the airports to accommodate them. A common mistake in many countries is to orient the system of higher education to the technology of the advanced countries rather than to practical and specific local needs.

Another basic problem is the failure to identify and to support effectively the most talented and creative people. The "uncommon man" with imagination, superior intelligence, and unusual energy should have better pay, higher status, and more recognition than the average man with education. High talent thrives on differential treatment rather than on application of common standards. Yet how to provide the necessary differentials—in working conditions, facilities, equipment, perquisites, associates, and pay—is a complex and often explosive question. Preferential treatment of high talent runs counter to strongly held egalitarian doctrines; it is inconsistent with traditional bureaucratic practice; and it is difficult to carry out because many people of mediocre talent also lay claim to special treatment. In most countries preferential treatment does exist, but it is based upon criteria such as ownership of land, income, or status often inherited from former colonial regimes. In short, providing the incentives for a development-minded meritocracy usually implies the downgrading of those who by custom or tradition have enjoyed preferred status, and this calls for very far-reaching social, economic, and political transformation.

It is important also for the talent elites to have a sense of community. Persons of high talent need to be productively interrelated. There must be enough of them—a critical mass—to interact. In scientific research, national planning, or cultural development, there must be concentrations of facilities, equipment, and people—centers of excellence—so that progressive viewpoints and new sets of values may be established and given continuity. But concentration points of high talent do not spring up automatically; in the developing countries they must be consciously created and systematically supported.

To be sure, the developing countries, even with the best policies and organizations, may not be able to stem completely the outflow of strategic brainpower. The effective demand for high talent is on the rise everywhere in the modern world. In many areas, physicians being the outstanding example, the advanced countries are not producing enough talent to meet their own needs, and thus they may continue to draw upon the resources of the underdeveloped countries. The brain drain is thus in part the consequence of forces beyond the control of the less developed countries. There is no reason to believe that the international market for brains will be any less competitive in the future.

The export of educated manpower, however, is not always undesirable; and in some cases it is even encouraged by governments. In cases where the higher education system continues to turn out more graduates than can be employed at home, outmigration may not seriously retard growth. To the extent that a country invests in education to strengthen the nation, outmigration clearly is a loss. But if its major objective is to benefit its citizens as individuals, the export of educated persons is more easily justified. In the case of the Philippines, for example, where medical schools are financed from fees of private individuals, the nation as a whole does not suffer from migration of doctors, particularly when there is insufficient effective demand for their services at home. Similar situations exist in the case of physicians and engineers in India. Developing countries, therefore, may not suffer acutely from drainage of the overflow of educated persons as long as they can retain adequate numbers of their talented manpower. In other cases, the developing countries may actually encourage, if not force, outmigration of talented people. This has been true in East Africa where pressure to leave is being put on Asians (for the most part aliens but in certain cases local citizens as well). In Kenya, Uganda, and Tanzania, Asians have held a dominating position in trade; they have been the traditional commercial entrepreneurs; and a great many have higher education in science, engineering, and other critical fields. They are being forced to leave through a variety of pressures—discrimination in allocation of opportunity for education, denial of work permits, licenses for business, and restriction of entry into government service. The resentment by the Africans of Asian influence is understandable; at the same time their expulsion in large numbers results in a serious drain of essential brainpower.

For any developing country, the building of an effective policy for the import and export of brainpower is a difficult task. The major paths of national development must be clearly specified, for they determine the parameters for scientific research, choice of technology, and high-talent manpower requirements. For example, if the development strategy calls for large modern factories, there will be a demand for engineers familiar with the latest technologies found in the advanced countries. Normally, these are the easiest to train since the content of an appropriate program of education is well known. Emphasis on small-scale enterprises using intermediate technology may require an entirely different kind of engineering manpower which may be much more difficult to develop. Emphasis on rural development will generate a need for agricultural scientists who are capable of applying new technologies to a wide variety of local conditions, and who are usually more difficult to develop. The amount of resources devoted to public health will determine the effective demand for physicians and medical technicians. Without a development strategy, no country can design a realistic program to retain and motivate its high-level human resources.

The loss of critical manpower through outmigration is in most cases an indication of an imbalance between a country's system of employment generation and its system of education. Like the exposed part of an iceberg, it is a manifestation of more basic and massive problems beneath the surface. An effective balance of brains is not likely to be achieved by imposing arbitrary restrictions on the out-migration of talent. Nor would the refusal of advanced nations to import talent from the Third World nations be of much practical benefit. No doubt the physical movement of manpower from one country to another could be restrained, but this would provide little incentive for the creative application of brainpower to the solution of critical problems.

THE INTERNATIONAL MIGRATION OF TALENT

Of equal significance for modernization is the migration of talent from the less developed rural areas to the more advanced modern enclaves within the developing countries. The movement of masses of unskilled labor from the countryside to the cities was discussed in Chapter 2. The related movement of highly educated people to the urban centers is likewise a matter of critical concern. Characteristically, bright young people migrate to the cities in search of education, and they are likely to remain in the modern sectors once they have acquired the education. Rural life provides few opportunities for educated persons. Despite the need for their services, there is little effective demand for doctors, qualified teachers, engineers, and organization-building entrepreneurs. The rural areas are usually too poor to support their activities.

The internal distribution of talent in most developing countries shows wide disparities. Mexico is perhaps a typical case in point, as Table I demonstrates.

It is clear from the table that doctors, teachers, and professional and scientific manpower are concentrated in the relatively advanced states which are the most highly urbanized and which also have the largest Gross State Product (that is, total production of goods and services in a state) per capita. The same is true for persons with secondary and post-secondary education. This pattern is typical of many other developing countries. The concentration of both educational facilities and employment opportunities for educated manpower in the advanced areas of the country results in a drain of the more

Table I Mexico: distribution of high-level manpower

	Per cent urban population	Gross state product per capita	Doctors per 10,000 population	Teachers 2nd and 3rd level per 10,000 population	Per cent total labor force listed as professionals, technicians, and managers	Educational attainment		
						9-12 years	13+ years	Mean (in years) 30+ years
	(1)	(2)	(3)	(4)	(5)	(6)	(7)	(8)
Relatively advanced states								
Federal District	100.0	853	15.06	49.3	10.5	12.1	4.9	4.6
Baja Calif.	71.0	662	9.52	8.7	6.2	5.4	1.2	3.4
Nuevo Leon	57.8	716	10.34	21.8	6.3	8.4	2.3	3.5
Tamaulipas	50.2	438	7.83	8.0	4.3	5.4	1.1	2.9
Coahuila	48.7	458	6.58	12.7	5.2	6.4	0.6	3.0
Chihuahua	40.3	380	5.28	9.7	4.5	4.5	0.9	2.9
Sonora	37.7	587	6.57	9.1	4.6	4.2	1.0	2.9
Relatively less developed states								
Hidalgo	9.2	121	2.61	5.0	2.4	1.7	0.3	1.3
Chiapas	8.7	135	2.48	4.6	1.9	1.0	0.2	1.1
Zacatecas	8.4	109	1.75	2.7	2.1	0.9	0.2	1.6
Guerrero	6.5	133	2.46	3.7	2.2	0.8	0.2	0.8
Oaxaca	5.3	86	1.44	4.5	1.7	0.8	0.2	1.0
Tlaxcala	0.0	88	2.19	5.6	3.1	1.5	0.2	1.7

SOURCE: Information in columns 1, 2, 3, 4, 6, and 7 calculated from data obtained from Charles N. Myers; in columns 5 and 8 from Charles N. Myers, *Education and National Development in Mexico* (Princeton: Industrial Relations Section, Princeton University, 1965), pp. 24 and 27.

capable and energetic elements from the less developed regions. This again is a common pattern in many developing countries.

It is difficult to prevent the flow of brainpower to the urban areas. The greater availability of secondary and higher education in rural areas might slow the migration of those young people who go to the cities in search of educational opportunities. On the other hand, rural-based schools, if oriented to modern-sector careers, could encourage even greater rural-urban migration. Some countries require doctors, teachers, and other highly trained personnel to work in rural areas for a specified period (usually one or two years) after completing their professional training, but the service performed by persons forced to work under such a regulation may be mediocre at best. Although men can be forced to serve time in rural areas, they cannot be compelled to be productive. Another measure, adopted in Ethiopia, is to require university students to spend a year in national service as part of the required academic program. Here the objective is to give students some practical understanding of rural problems and, it is hoped, to stimulate their interest in careers related to rural development. For the same purpose universities in other countries are employing students on rural-related research projects. The effectiveness of all of these measures, however, is largely untested.

In the final analyses, the most logical means of controlling the rural-urban brain drain is to provide more challenging jobs and better working conditions for high-talent manpower in the rural areas. The wide range of programs for generating more employment opportunities in rural areas was discussed at length in Chapter 2. Any attempt to bring about a rural transformation through concentrating exclusively on changing the structure and orientation of formal education offers no real solution. Indeed the expansion of educational opportunity without a corresponding growth of employment opportunity in rural areas is more likely to stimulate rather than stem the outmigration of brains. As in the case of the drain of brains to advanced countries, the internal rural-urban drain is a surface manifestation of a much more fundamental imbalance between a country's system of employment generation and its system for developing human resources.

6 | National Development from the Human Resources Perspective

In the preceding chapters the major problems of development and utilization of human resources have been identified. They were discussed under four general categories: (1) those related to employment generation and the utilization of the labor force in productive activity; (2) those connected with the development of skills, knowledge, and capacities of people through the formal education system; (3) those pertaining to skill development through nonformal education and training activities; and (4) those associated with the internal and international migration of strategic high-talent manpower. A more formal approach will be to view these four problem areas as separate systems, each of which is interrelated with the other, as shown in Figure 1.

These four systems can provide a developing country with a framework for collection, classification, and analysis of pertinent data. They afford an orderly means of filing pertinent information, and the information in each category may then provide the basis for analysis. It is possible, for example, to analyze the system of employment generation in terms of the capacity of the economy to produce jobs and the nature and extent of unemployment, underemployment, and other manifestations of underutilization in various sectors. The formal education system can be analyzed with respect to outputs, access, orientation, and resource constraints. The most important characteristics of the nonformal system likewise may be studied with particular emphasis on its relationship to the formal schooling process and

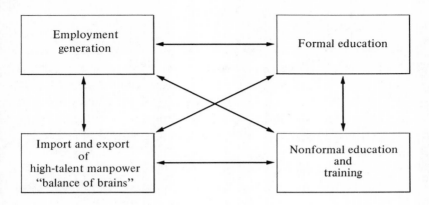

Figure 1

the linkages to employment generation. And the export and import of high-talent manpower, both in terms of internal and external migration, can be subjected to systematic review. These four systems are interrelated. The employment generation system will affect the formal education system as well as the migration of high-talent manpower and vice versa. The informal and formal systems of education and training are closely related and may be considered as constituent elements or subdivisions of the broader nationwide learning system. And, as noted in Chapter 5, the migration of talent is in large measure a reflection of maladjustment or ineffective gearing between the employment generation system and those of formal and nonformal education.

Human resources problems may be examined from different perspectives. Social scientists, for example, view the process of modernization in varying ways, reflecting their assumptions of what is of central or trivial importance as well as their disciplinary bias. This means that there can be many different logical frameworks for national development, each concentrating on different goals. The human resources approach is one.

Orthodox economic doctrine holds that growth is primarily a process of accumulating material wealth. Economic progress is measured by the production of goods and services, expressed for the most part in monetary terms. The growth process generates employment for the labor force and also specifies the demand for a hierarchy of occupational skills and knowledge. From this perspective, unemployment and other manifestations of underutilization of human resources are mainly the consequence of an insufficient rate of economic growth. This logic holds that these problems can best be resolved by accelerating the accumulation of material wealth. Better housing, better nutrition, better health, and many of the other good things in life are all made possible by increasing a nation's income, and it should thus be the supreme target of national growth.

The GNP approach would opt for maximum income growth even if concentrated in small but highly productive leading sectors of the economy. Progress in such sectors is counted on to trickle down in time to the masses in the intermediate and traditional sectors. Meanwhile, subsistence agriculture can provide a huge storage reservoir for the bulk of the labor force until such time as they can be drawn into more highly productive activities in the rural and urban modern sectors. In its simplest formulation, the GNP approach assumes that, for most countries, economic development mandates the transferring of rural labor to urban employment with higher productivity and incomes. The underutilization of human resources in the transition period is not a matter of great concern, nor is the distribution of income between the rich and the poor. It is believed that such disparities will diminish in the long run if there is sufficient growth in aggregate income.

Adherents to the GNP approach do not deny the existence of serious human resources problems as development proceeds. But these are seen as somewhat temporary side effects—acceptable costs—of the development process. Where possible, unemployment should be reduced and the misery of the masses alleviated, but not in such a way as to slow down the accumulation of aggregate wealth. For, as the logic dictates, a country must first become rich before it can cope with the lamentations of the poor.

Our approach rests on a different premise. It holds that human resources, not material wealth as such, are the ultimate basis of wealth. The goal of development is thus maximum possible utilization of human resources in more productive activity and fullest possible development of the skills and knowledge of the labor force which are relevant to such activity. The production of useful goods and services thus becomes a logical consequence of utilization and development of human resources. This approach stresses the importance of utilizing *all* human resources in productive activity and developing skills, knowledge, and capacities of the *entire* labor force. The reduction of unemployment is thought to be a central arm of development policy, for to reduce unemployment is to raise consumption levels, especially of those who are most in need. The development effort, moreover, should not be concentrated, solely or even mainly, on a few leading sectors. Small per capita improvement of the masses in the labor force is considered to be just as important in the aggregate as spectacular advances in the modern-sector enclaves. The human resources approach stresses the reduction of inequality of opportunity. And, in addition to providing more material wealth, it includes better health, better nutrition, and wider involvement in the processes of modernization as high-priority end results of national development.

The human resources approach makes three assumptions. First, in developing countries, human resources are the most plentiful of all resources and, for the most part, they are grossly underutilized. Second, the skills, knowledge, and capacities of the labor force are capable of almost limitless growth, and in most countries they are developed far short of their practical potential. And third, even lacking liberal endowments of natural resources and material capital, the less developed countries can prosper by maximizing the productive utilization and effective development of their labor forces.

Both the GNP and human resources approaches are essentially economic perspectives, but neither denies the importance of non-economic factors in broadly based national development. Both, for example, recognize that education has purposes other than preparing persons to participate in the labor force. Neither will deny the value of cultural development, the building of a sense of community, the role of ideologies in nation-building. In economic policy, the GNP and human resources approaches may be thought to be in conflict, but this is not always the case. Both associate higher levels of material wealth with progress. The GNP approach holds that opportunities for employment and learning stem from increased output; the human resources approach maintains that increased output is the result rather than the means of broadening employment and learning opportunities.

Economists have often raised the question of whether maximum production is consistent with maximum employment. Sweeten and Stewart, for example, in a penetrating discussion of the complexities of relationships between the two, conclude that in many cases the path which maximizes the growth in output may also be that which maximizes employment growth.[1] Gustav Ranis, in looking at Asian economies is more specific as the following statement indicates.

We have evidence . . . that growth without conflict with employment apparently could be achieved not only in historical Japan, but also in contemporary Taiwan, Korea, and West Pakistan. If we look at the development performance of these countries in some perspective, we can at least make the general observation that they were able to achieve rapid rates of growth because of, rather than in spite of, a very labor intensive, therefore employment-creating, type of development strategy. In other words, far from being antithetical to each other, it may well be that the main ingredient of these so-called success stories is this very ability to move towards employment and output maximization at the same time.[2]

1. Frances Stewart and Paul Sweeten, "Conflicts Between Output and Employment Objectives in Developing Countries," *Oxford Economic Papers,* Vol. 23, No. 2 (July 1971), pp. 145-68.
2. Gustav Ranis, "Output and Employment in the 70's: Conflict or Complements," in *Employment and Unemployment Problems of Southeast and South Asia,* edited by Ronald G. Ridker and Harold Lubell (New Delhi: Vikas Publications, 1971), Vol. I, p. 61.

The "supreme targets" of the GNP and human resources approaches are, of course, quite different. Some matters of central concern in the human resources approach, such as skill and knowledge development, are really tangential to the GNP perspective. But in many areas, such as employment generation, the main difference appears to be in assumptions of cause and effect.

The terminology of the human resources approach needs to be specified with some precision.

The "maximum possible utilization of human resources in more productive activity" requires some elaboration. Productive activity includes work in subsistence agriculture, modern farming, small- and large-scale industry as well as commerce, government service, and education. In our definition it also extends to the work of actors, artists, musicians, journalists, writers, poets, religious leaders, and others whose services to society are not always appropriately valued in narrow definitions of GNP. These and many others are members of the labor force who engage in productive or useful activity. The development of the capacities of people, therefore, most certainly is not confined to persons who produce material things.

For the subsistence farmer "more productive activity" can mean improvement in the quality and quantity of food grown, better housing, some access to health services, and other manifestations of better living even if he still remains largely outside of the monetized economy. And, in both rural and urban areas, more productive activity implies more opportunity for employment and higher income in the monetized sectors. For the self-employed it implies greater opportunity for providing services for compensation. More productive activity is a relative term, implying greater opportunity relative to one's previous condition. For example, a modest increase in a peasant's food supply may be quite as meaningful to him as a large boost in salary will be to a wealthy civil servant. Basically the human resources perspective stresses some broadening of opportunity for *all* elements in the labor force, and progress is conceived to be movement toward a multiopportunity or multioption society.

The term "maximum possible utilization" means the fullest employment of human resources which is practically consistent with a country's level of development. Employment opportunities are subject to constraints of availability of land, mineral resources, and capital as well as highly skilled and knowledgeable manpower and effective organization of productive activity. As also in the GNP perspective, development progresses slowly along a constrained path strewn with formidable obstacles.

"The fullest possible development of the skills and knowledge of the labor force" is best described as the maximization of learning opportunities which are relevant to if not required for realistic participation of members of the labor force in productive activity. Learning opportunities are provided through formal education (outlined in Chapter 3) and informal education and training (described in Chapter 4). Logically, the human resources approach stresses employment-oriented learning, but this is interpreted broadly. In accordance with the definition of productive activity given above, the study of the arts and humanities may be just as employment-oriented as engineering or natural science. And, of course, out-of-school learning can be just as relevant to productive activity as formal schooling.

Investment in learning develops the capability of the labor force to engage in evermore complicated productive activity which in turn increases the level of employment opportunity. And higher levels of employment opportunity raise the demand for persons with higher levels of learning. Thus, employment opportunity and learning opportunity feed each other. The human resources approach is centrally concerned with the effective interrelationship or gearing between the two.

GENERATION OF PRODUCTIVE EMPLOYMENT IN RURAL
AND URBAN AREAS

The goal of the human resources approach is a full-employment economy in which all members of the labor force will have some share of the fruits of more productive activity. At best this is a long-range goal, and, in countries with high rates of population increase, it may be impossible to attain. But it does specify the proper direction of development—toward full employment. The planning effort, therefore, starts with the setting of sectoral employment targets.

In most developing countries with rapidly rising populations, the bulk of the labor force is in the rural areas and will be there for several decades to come. Estimation of the absorptive capacity for rural labor is thus of primary importance. In most cases the major concern will be not to release labor from the land but to find ways of employing it more productively in rural areas. The objective of development is thus to increase the *opportunity-generating* capacity of the rural sectors. This requires consideration of several development programs: expansion of labor-intensive commercial agriculture, improvement in levels of living in subsistence agriculture, promotion of rurally based industry and commerce, and large-scale investment in rationally planned public works. To strengthen all of these it is necessary to have a consistent policy of incentives and taxation.

The human resources as well as the GNP approach would give high priority to discovery and application of advanced technology in agriculture, forestry, animal husbandry, and related activities. It would stress use of new seeds, fertilizers, pesticides, and irrigation to improve both the quantity and quality of production of both export and food crops. However, it would restrict labor-saving mechanization. The human resources approach would generally favor small family-operated farms over large holdings. It would press vigorously land reform where it would be required to enable larger numbers of persons to engage in commercial agriculture. And this would call for substantial expansion of rural learning services such as agricultural extension and farmer training.

In most countries, it is probably not possible to increase the total number of persons engaged in commercial agriculture. With rising productivity and incomes in this sector, the most that can be expected is to prevent the displacement of labor by large landholders using labor-saving technology. Net employment expansion would result, it is hoped, from the multiplier effect of increases in farm incomes and from expansion in public works and services.

It is doubtful whether the aggregate number of subsistence farmers can be reduced in view of the high rates of increase in labor forces which are expected in most countries during the next few decades. In the human resources approach, however, some effort would be made to improve the quality of life in the traditional sector. With appropriate assistance, both the quantity and quality of food production may be increased. Modest improvements may be made in primitive housing and homecrafts, sanitation, and water supplies. In other words, the work of the subsistence peasant may be lightened and his productivity increased without full entry into the monetary economy. Whereas the GNP yardstick might ignore the subsistence farmer completely, the human resources approach would emphasize improving his productivity and finding a means of including his increased opportunity in the measures of development progress.

In both the GNP and human resources approaches, the expansion of credit and marketing services, enterprises supplying farm inputs such as fertilizer, seeds, and implements, village crafts, and small commercial business would be an expected consequence of higher incomes in commercial farming. The building of plants to process agricultural products would be of major interest in each. Both would count on these activities to generate a substantial volume of new opportunities for absorbing rural labor.

Investment in public works and extension of public services would be expected to absorb a good part of the annual increase in the labor forces remaining in rural areas. The building of roads, irrigation canals, water supply systems, food storage facilities, and training centers all contribute directly to expansion of agriculture and commercial activity. An increase in services such as education, farmer training, agricultural extension, and public health would also be strategic elements in broadly based rural development. Both public works and public services, fortunately, are usually quite labor-intensive but, in the human resources perspective, they should be developed in accord with the following principles.

First, under no circumstances should investment be made in public works and public services solely to increase employment. The building of monuments, roads which lead nowhere, or vocational schools to produce unmarketable skills, while perhaps temporarily increasing employment, do not constitute productive use of human resources. Public works and service activities should be undertaken only if they are essential for development of other employment-generating productive activities. They should be integral elements of a strategy for rural development and not accessories to it tacked on subsequently for job creation purposes.

Second, public works and service programs wherever possible should utilize labor-intensive rather than capital-intensive technologies. If there is a choice of technology, the one which provides the most employment opportunity consistent with effective operations should be chosen.

Finally, as far as possible, jobs in rural public works and services should be reserved for those already in the rural labor force. This is justified on two grounds: first, to increase the opportunity horizons for the rural labor force and thus stem migration to the cities; second, to avoid reliance on more educated city dwellers (such as school teachers and doctors) who are reluctant to accept employment in rural areas for sustained periods of time.

Appropriate taxation and incentives can be used to encourage a labor-intensive pattern of rural development. Through subsidies and taxes, for example, the prices of labor-saving machinery may be raised and those of tube wells and simpler implements reduced. Small farms could be given tax advantages over larger holdings. Above all, income generated in rural areas should be channeled into rural rather than urban development. Rural inhabitants will be willing to devote resources, either in labor or in taxes, for projects from which they can derive clear benefits. They will co-operate to construct schools, dig wells and build access roads, improve land and cultivate it more intensively, if they are assured the major share of the increased output. However, it is unrealistic to treat agriculture as a major source of revenue for investment in industrialization and urban development and at the same time to expect more private investment of time and resources in agriculture.

The package of policies suggested above, if followed consistently in most countries, could increase employment opportunities and levels of living in the rural areas. The expected consequence would be an expansion in rural incomes shared widely throughout the population which might be quite effective in reducing migration to the cities. And as a result of rural income generation, the markets for goods produced in the urban areas would be expanded at the same time.

The allocation of resources to opportunity generation in rural areas is likely to impose limits on modern-sector urban development. Yet, it need not retard the rate of employment expansion and industrial development. Indeed, some stringency in the availability of capital might even stimulate employment through changes in factor prices which would encourage more labor-intensive technologies.

In the human resources perspective, industrialization would be spearheaded by small and medium sized enterprises using capital-saving rather than labor-displacing technologies. Priority would be given to producers of "wage goods" which are purchased in abundance by the middle- and lower-income classes and also to labor-intensive export industries. Both the capital per output and output per employment ratios can be relatively low if based upon innovative, modern technology appropriate for countries with abundant human resources and scarce capital resources. The successful experiences of Taiwan and Korea with labor-intensive export-oriented industries was noted in Chapter 2. In historical perspective, much of Japan's industrial development likewise was characterized by encouragement of small-scale enterprise, substitution of labor for capital in manufacturing processes, and ingenious promotion of export markets. The key for success in labor-intensive industrial development is aggressive entrepreneurship and imaginative technological adaptation.

In both the GNP and human resource perspectives, emphasis on import-substitution industries would be questioned. Many are capital-intensive; most require tariff protection at least initially; few provide much additional employment in the long run. However, most developing countries have a propensity to favor import-substitution industries through a combination of overvalued exchange rates, low interest rates, and favorable internal terms of trade for industry, all with the objective of protecting modern-sector industrial development which is highly capital-intensive. There may be several reasons for this: modern factories are impressive symbols of growth; the technology is easily available in the advanced countries; the organizational and manpower requirements are clearly specified so that the training of the work force is relatively simple; and in many cases external aid is available. Yet, the import-substitution industries serve only a limited internal market; in few countries do they employ more than a tiny fraction of the urban labor force; and they siphon off a lion's share of the country's scarce capital resources. Thus, the countries which have the most ostentatious modern-sector growth are seldom the ones which are maximizing growth of GNP or employment. Others, notably again Korea and Taiwan, which have pursued policies which are more in line with their factor endowments, have done much better in achieving high levels of economic growth and near full employment. This argument can be bolstered by quoting again from Ranis:

What I am, in fact, suggesting is that the general experience of the 50's and 60's which indicates the existence of a severe conflict in terms of rising output and unemployment levels is entirely misleading because the very strategy which was followed in the pursuit of output maximization was erroneous while a different set of policies might well have given us more growth *and* more employment. As economists and perpetrators of the dismal science, we seem to have difficulty in accepting the notion that it is possible to have more of both, i.e., more output and more employment. It is an incontrovertible fact that a substantial part of the profession and an even larger majority of policy makers implicitly or explicitly assume the existence of a conflict and are proceeding to talk about employment strategies as a way to ameliorate or amend the "output only" policies of the past. They talk about dethroning the GNP on behalf of employment and distribution. My point is that it may well come to that, but it may also be true that we have not even begun to explore a set of policies and development strategies which would give us increased output as a direct consequence of utilizing our unemployed or underemployed labor more effectively.[3]

3. *Ibid.,* p. 61.

In the area of incomes policy, the human resources and GNP approaches would not be in conflict. On social and political grounds, neither would suggest that wages of urban labor be lowered to their logical equilibrium levels. Both, however, recognize that rapidly rising wages and salaries in government and modern-sector employment will generate pressure for greater use of labor-saving technology and at the same time magnify the drawing power for migrants from the rural areas who will be unable to find employment. The human resources approach, however, might put more emphasis on the reduction of disparities between rich and poor, urban and rural dwellers, and industrial and agricultural workers. It would logically favor restraint of large increases in earnings of a very small minority of persons employed in the modern sector.

As is commonly known, construction is by nature a labor-intensive activity, and it has sufficient technological flexibility to allow wide-ranging substitution of men for machines. In the urban areas of developing countries, it often is a larger employer of manpower than manufacturing. Without question, public works are important generators of employment. The crucial question here is the choice between additional urban or more rural public works. Since the developing countries have a propensity anyway to invest in the cities, it is probable that both the GNP and human resources approaches would favor some shifting to rural public works.

In summary, it is possible for developing countries, following logical policies, to have industrial and urban development which will generate substantial employment. Yet, it would be unrealistic to assume that such development can provide the major solution for the problem of underutilization of human resources. The manufacturing sectors are but small islands in the economies of Third World nations, employing at best only about 5 to 10 per cent of the labor force. It is doubtful, indeed, whether manufacturing and construction combined in the urban areas can absorb more than a fraction of the annual increase in the labor force. Until such time as growth in population declines to the levels of the presently advanced countries, most of the labor surplus will have to be absorbed in the countryside rather than in the cities.

DEVELOPMENT OF SKILLS AND KNOWLEDGE
OF THE LABOR FORCE

The GNP approach has little to offer for policy guidance in the area of development of human skills. It recognizes the scarcity of skilled and knowledgeable manpower, along with capital and natural resources, as a constraint on growth. In theory it might suggest that the allocation of resources to training and education be based upon a cost-benefit analysis of these contributions to national income, but in view of both the data and methodological problems involved, few planners are likely in practice to rely on such analysis. Indeed, the strict "GNP constructionist" is more likely to banish education to the field of social development, which is too amorphous and intangible for systematic quantitative analysis.

In the human resources approach, however, development of skills, knowledge, and capacities of the labor force is the sum and substance of accumulation of wealth. Investment in man is the supreme target. This concept is appealing to educationists who might advocate massive increases in expenditures on formal education starting with the earliest possible achievement of universal primary education and expanding the higher levels of schooling to accommodate the growing demand for evermore education. As discussed in Chapter 3, however, the expansion of education on a "more of the same" basis is likely to result in widespread unemployment or underemployment of educated persons in most developing countries. Formal education has an important role to play in human resources development, but it is only one of several essential skill-generating processes of modern nations.

The human resources approach would attempt to maximize continuous *recurrent* learning opportunities throughout man's working life which are relevant for more productive employment. It would stress: (1) improvement of the skill and knowledge-generating capacity of working environments; (2) provision of productive training services for adults through a wide variety of job-related programs; and (3) broadly based formal education which, while not oriented to producing specific skills, would develop at all levels perceptive and knowledgeable persons capable of entering the widest possible range of occupations.

Although not questioning the ideal of universal primary education, the human resources approach would stress a broader goal: universal opportunity for learning of some kind which would increase the effectiveness of everyone—adults as well as children—as participants in the labor force. It would hold that a young adult who has never been to school should have some other opportunity for learning, and that this person, even if illiterate, is capable of learning new methods through extension services and properly designed training centers. For social and political, as well as economic, reasons, every man, woman, and child should be thought of as a potential "learning station." In the human resources perspective, the opportunity to learn is a human right which would be given higher priority than the opportunity for every child to attend school for a specified period of time.

There are many ways to improve the skill-generating capacities of working environments. More intensive utilization of the training potential of large expatriate enterprises could serve as an example. Foreign-owned manufacturing enterprises, automobile and equipment distributors, and large commercial establishments usually can do a better job of training in a wide range of skills than locally owned enterprises or vocational schools. Under certain conditions governments could maximize the contribution of expatriate enterprises to skill development by requiring them to train a surplus beyond their immediate needs. Also more pressure could be put on these enterprises to accelerate the preparation of local nationals for the higher level technical and managerial positions.

Another possibility is to expand and improve in-service training in government services. Governments of newly developing countries are large employers of manpower. They probably have more potential skill-generating capacity than enterprises in the private sector. Thus, in the human resources perspective, government ministries would be held responsible not only for providing public services but also for increasing the skills and capabilities of civil servants.

Also, technical services can be supplied to farmers and small enterprises to improve their own skills and·also to train their employees and associates better. Agricultural extension in rural areas is an obvious example. Parallel services for small and medium manufacturing and commercial establishments can be equally effective.

The examples cited certainly do not exhaust the range of possibilities for expanding the skill-generating function of working environments. The human resources approach would give high priority to assessment of the skill-generating potential of every kind of working environment, and it would allocate substantial resources to improvement of the skill-generating process.

The provision of productive education and training services for adults needs little elaboration. The range of possibilities for consideration is vast. Among the more obvious are farmer training centers, work-oriented adult literacy, rural polytechnics, nutrition and health centers, employer-financed training and apprenticeship organizations such as SENA, and many others mentioned in Chapter 4. If properly developed, these services can reach large numbers of people. In some cases they may be a substitute for formal education; in others they can be a means of building upon it. Although most of these services are underdeveloped, scattered, and unco-ordinated, they perform vital functions and may well justify a larger share of the resources available for providing learning opportunities.

The functions and problems of formal education were discussed in detail in Chapter 3 and need little elaboration here. Formal education provides the base upon which many other learning services must be built. In most countries it probably consumes more resources than all other learning services combined. Without question, the resources allocated to it will increase. But there is need for a logical re-examination of its role in the universe of learning opportunities. The crucial question is how much of the emphasis of first- and second-level education should be placed on preparation for more education and how much of it should be oriented toward direct entry into the world of work.

As the capstone of the education system, the university will play a strategic role in any nationwide learning system. It can press forward research and development of knowledge which is relevant to the critical problems of national development, or it can become an ivory tower of inwardly directed contemplation. It can transmit useful knowledge to students, or it can simply function as a monopoly for issuing pass cards for entry into the ranks of the elite. The university may lead or follow the march of development, or it can advance or retard the pace. And since it consumes such a large proportion of resources to provide benefits for such a tiny percentage of the students, the university should be subject to more critical examination than any of the other learning activities in the nationwide system.

Guiding principles for building a broad learning system would be: (1) comparative advantage; (2) multipurpose services; (3) decentralized planning and administration; and (4) rational allocation of funding for all constituent learning programs.

The identification of the comparative advantages of various learning systems requires careful analysis. For example, formal education is best suited to extending cognitive knowledge. At the lower levels its primary mission is to teach children to read, write, and calculate. At higher levels it imparts knowledge of language, arts, humanities, science, and technology. Its comparative advantage is in developing the mind, the ability to think, the capacity to make rational choices, and the understanding of the culture and environment of society.

Many developing countries expect far too much from formal education. They want it to produce skills which are learned much better on the job. They hope that it will produce managers, administrators, and statesmen, without realizing that such persons really acquire most of their skills in the crucible of experience on the job. As a rule the strength of formal education does not lie in training manual craftsmen, factory workers, or modern farmers. Here, employing institutions and employment-oriented nonformal training have a decided advantage. Also farmer training centers may be more effective in some situations than agricultural extension. Work-oriented literacy programs are usually more useful than formal courses are in teaching adults. And national industrial training schemes, such as SENA in

Colombia, can be better than vocational schools in building middle-level skills required in the modern sector.

A national learning system must provide a great variety of learning opportunities. They vary by country, region, locality, occupation, and eligibility. A major task of human resources planning is to provide an appropriate package of learning services for each area. Tanzania has this in mind in its plan for building model community schools in rural villages. These schools will offer formal primary education for school-age children, and they will also be centers for adult literacy classes and discussion groups and other training programs. Each will have a "practical room" where both children and adults can learn handicrafts, carpentry, and other simple skills, and in each there will be a community kitchen and dining room, a library (serviced by mobile units), and radio, film strips, and visual aids. The objective is to make the schools into community "hubs" providing, under one roof, a variety of basic learning services for young and old. Teachers are trained to work with adults as well as children, and even primary school leavers are employed to conduct adult literacy programs. The central concept of the model school is to prepare people for more productive lives in their communities through making learning a common concern of working families as well as a special activity for children. There is a limit, however, to the services which can be effectively provided by community schools. Other institutions such as district training centers for farming skills and more sophisticated crafts are usually required to fill out the range of services which may be required.

Decentralized planning and administration are necessary in order to provide flexibility and to generate support and enthusiasm for local learning programs, but in most countries this may encounter strong opposition. The ministries responsible for providing learning services, such as agriculture, education, and labor are likely to have vested interests in nationwide programs. Their local functionaries are prone to work vertically with their superiors in the national ministries rather than horizontally as members of local teams. The allocation of resources for different programs is made centrally not locally.

Without control over resource allocation and with government officials who take their orders from above, the practical possibilities of integrating learning services is limited. Also there may be a dearth of persons capable of undertaking the critical planning and administrative tasks. The effective development of comprehensive learning services at regional and local levels, therefore, poses a major problem in public administration.

The rational allocation of resources to various learning activities depends on the assessment of comparative advantage, the mix of multiple services required in different rural or urban areas, and the local planning and administrative capacity. Ideally, this would rest on cost-benefit studies of the effectiveness of various programs, assessment of alternative means for providing particular services, as well as firm knowledge about existing and future employment opportunities. In most countries, little consideration has been given to these matters. There may be extensive planning in education ministries for expansion of formal education, but this seldom involves much analysis of employment opportunities for school leavers and almost never extends to the wide range of nonformal training activities carried on by other ministries or private groups. In theory at least, the human resources approach would suggest that there be budgeting each year for all productive learning services, including formal education as a major but by no means exclusive means of development of skills and knowledge. The common measure of effectiveness would be relevant employment opportunities defined in the broadest possible terms.

The human resources approach thus envisages the creation of comprehensive and cohesive learning systems comprising all education and training activities, formal and nonformal, and the offer of some kind of learning service for everyone in the society. It also lays great stress on the importance of recurrent learning processes. In practice, developing countries have never undertaken such a task; most would have difficulty even in making an inventory of all existing learning activities. There are as yet no reliable means of measuring the comparative effectiveness of various programs; in most cases, any such attempt to breach the lines of command of established ministries would fuel opposition from entrenched bureaucrats.

On the other hand, the human resources perspective does provide directional markers. Perhaps no country can ever have a truly comprehensive and completely cohesive learning system, but progress may be made toward that goal. Traditionally, the developing countries have directed their attention primarily to formal education. More recently, they have become aware of the vast but largely unharnessed potential of nonformal training activities. In the future they are likely to discover the benefits to be won by better integration of both.

THE EASY AND THE HARD TASKS

National development moves forward along an obstacle course, and many of the human resources problems to be encountered have been described in this and the preceding chapters. Some may be easily resolved; others may be virtually insolvable, at least within the next few decades. Here are some tentative generalizations.

By and large, it is much easier to develop skills and knowledge in the labor force than to provide productive opportunities for employment. This was not true in the case of the presently advanced countries primarily because they were not overburdened by high rates of growth in population. In the presently developing countries, the labor surplus resulting from rising population growth is probably the most important cause of underutilization of human resources. In the long run, the limitation of population growth will be the most effective means of reducing unemployment and underemployment to acceptable levels.

In the short run, the rural areas must provide the bulk of new employment opportunities. In the Third World countries, over two-thirds of the labor force is engaged in rural activity; the job expansion capacity of industry in the urban areas is limited, even taking into account the possibilities for developing labor-intensive export manufacturing. Unfortunately, the task of organizing programs to generate more rural employment is more difficult than that of organizing urban industry and modern-sector expansion. The requirements and techniques for the latter are fairly well known; they are largely unexplored or underdeveloped in the former. Thus, for most countries, rural transformation will be a more formidable task than industrial development.

The developing nations are committing substantial funds to formal education and are likely to allocate more of their resources to it in the future. Here the problem is not underinvestment but rather the failure to define the most appropriate role for formal education within the constellation of learning services which are relevant to employment opportunities. It is relatively easy to educate and train people for modern-sector employment. The organization tables and skill requirements for government bureaucracies and large enterprises are well known. High-level manpower can be imported to fill temporary deficiencies. Formal education which is oriented primarily to modern-sector development normally produces more than enough "trainable" candidates for employment and the requisite skills can be developed on the job without great difficulty.

In contrast, it is more difficult to educate and train manpower for productive rural activity. The organizational arrangements and required skills are hard to specify. High-talent manpower cannot be borrowed from advanced countries. Formal education directs the attention of the young away from agriculture and rural life. And in-service training of masses of small farmers is vastly more costly than training large groups of workers in factories or commercial enterprises.

At the same time, the developing countries may take comfort in the fact that practically every problem of human resources development can be solved through some kind of learning process. Man's capacity for productive work is almost limitless, given appropriate inputs of education and training. Most developing countries can overcome specifically defined skill and knowledge bottlenecks within relatively short time periods. And within reason, nearly all developing countries are capable of undertaking national development programs requiring sizable inputs of sophisticated and high-talent manpower. Thus, if the development of human resources is the ultimate basis of wealth, all countries may prosper by judicious investment in man.

The most perplexing of all human resources problems, however, is organization. Organization is required to mobilize the energies of the labor force. It is necessary to create a state, to build economic and political institutions, to propagate ideologies, and thus to carry forward every aspect of national development. Organization is the co-ordinated effort of many persons toward common objectives. Its structure is almost inevitably a hierarchy of superiors and subordinates in which the higher levels exercise authority over the lower levels. The successful leaders of organizations, or more precisely the organization-builders, are a small but aggressive minority who feed the aspirations, give expression to the goals, and shape the destinies of people. In the human resources perspective, organization-building is the most critical of all tasks for national development. Good organization makes it possible to maximize employment and learning opportunities; poor organization can perpetuate the underdevelopment and underutilization of the capacities of man. Unfortunately, there is no ready-made formula for producing organization-builders; the organizational architecture of advanced countries may be quite unsuitable for the developing nations. The developing countries, for the most part, will have to design and develop their own. The hope is that provision of learning opportunities and the emphasis on the human element in development processes will bring forth a growing number of persons with entrepreneurial, managerial, and organization-building skills. Implicit in the human resources perspective, hope is always considered to be more logical than despair.

7 | Problems of Implementation

Although in many areas the appropriate policy actions stemming from the GNP and human resources approaches may be the same, they specify different priorities, require different measures of progress, and place emphasis on different kinds of analysis. They also lead to different strategies of planning. These differences are explored in this chapter.

QUANTITATIVE MEASURES OF PROGRESS

A great virtue of the GNP approach is its adaptability to quantitative measurement. Economists have developed the techniques for measuring the value of aggregate production of goods and services, and most countries have made at least a start in collecting the kind of data required. Both the data and techniques are far from perfect, and questions can be raised about the accuracy of the measurement. In any case, the GNP approach offers a widely accepted means for keeping "score" on progress.

In the human resources approach, progress would have to be gauged not by one single measure but by a profile of indicators. As in modern medicine where the condition of the blood is determined by a battery of tests, so should the development and utilization of human resources be appraised by several different yardsticks. A measure of national income—GNP or GDP—would be one indicator of progress but not the supreme target. Others, conceivably, would be the following.

1. *An index of utilization of human resources*

The collection of statistics on employment, unemployment, and underemployment (in terms of hours worked) in the wage-earning part of the economy poses no serious problem. Here the concepts are essentially those which are widely used in advanced countries. However, the estimate of utilization or underutilization of persons in agriculture or in subsistence sectors in both rural and urban areas is much more difficult. Some sort of incomes approach could be attempted to measure the number of people at work and the hours worked, but it would also have to determine the productivity of such work in terms of income per hour. There would thus be two indicators for the nonmodern sectors: one of labor utilization (number of people at work and the number of hours worked) and the other of efficiency of work, for the goal of the human resources approach is not simply more hours of work but rather a decent standard of living for all, whether expressed in real or monetary terms. Admittedly, however, this kind of information would be very hard to collect because it involves sample household surveys of hours worked, type of work, output, and other factors.[1]

1. There are two experiments of special interest in this connection. The first is the Additional Rural Incomes Survey being performed for A.I.D. by the Indian National Council for Applied Economic Research. Conducted with a sample of 5000 over a three-year period and on a *household* (not individual) basis, this survey will provide information on the number of hours worked, types of jobs, incomes generated (as well as what happened to those incomes), and inputs in terms of hired and working capital and education. It is hoped that this ambitious project will give the Indian government a clearer picture of how rural people earn a living and what the most important keys to raising productivity *and* increasing the numbers of jobs are.

The second attempt to quantify the underutilization of human resources was presented by Philip Hauser at the Singapore Conference in May 1971. Initially, this was an elaboration of manpower surveys designed to count not only those working for wages but also self-employed and unpaid workers either inside or outside the household. The number of hours worked and availability for additional work were also to be included. Conference participants convinced Hauser that such surveys would be more useful on a household basis with questions about income added. Six countries in Southeast Asia are now experimenting with amended forms of the Hauser questionnaire under the overall guidance of the Committee for Asian Manpower Studies.

Thus, the utilization index would be based upon easily identifiable employment and unemployment data in the modern sector and estimates of the level of real income for large numbers of nonwage earning members of the labor force. The first would stem from reasonably hard data; the second might have to be estimated through sample surveys, informal conjecture, and even impressions. It is a possibility, moreover, that these could not be combined in a single index; in this case, there would be two indices of utilization.

2. *An index of health*

Health would be an important component of any human profile. However, its quantitative measurement is difficult. Life expectancy at birth as used in Chapter 1 could be a crude indicator. A better index would also include data on incidence of critical diseases, access to health facilities, and infant mortality. The major problem for most countries is availability of statistics, but this is of course true for all kinds of quantitative data.

3. *An index of nutrition*

Like health, nutrition is germane to effective development and utilization of human resources. Our index in Chapter 1, even though crude and arbitrary, could be improved upon by nutrition experts. The problem again is availability of relevant data.

4. *An index of skill and knowledge development*

Both conceptually and datawise, this would be the most difficult of all measures to devise. Theoretically, it should have two components: an indicator of the stock of skills in the labor force and an indicator of the skill-generating capacity of the learning system.

Some proxies may be found to measure stock. For example, statistics on formal educational attainment are available in many countries and can be collected in others. The number of physicians, engineers, scientists, and qualified teachers per 10,000 in the population are possible proxies for the stock of high-level manpower. But formal schooling does not reflect skills acquired on the job or through nonformal programs. Professional identification may simply express the extent of credentialization rather than the degree of skill and knowledge. And neither years of schooling nor professional identification provides information about the effectiveness of utilization of skilled manpower. The measurement of "flow" or generating capacity encounters similar difficulties. Enrollment ratios at all levels of formal education are usually readily available, but they tell nothing about the quality or orientation of the education system or how well it may be geared to employment opportunity. The skills generated in the working environment and by nonformal training activities probably cannot be estimated in any precise way. Some day, perhaps, an ingenious mind may invent a way to express "GLP" (Gross Learning Product) in quantitative terms. But in the meantime, both the extent of learning and the capacity to generate it must be assessed by qualitative judgment, if not intuitive reasoning.

5. *A measurement of disparities*

A cardinal principle of the human resources approach is that employment and learning opportunity should be extended to all segments of the population and that the "level of living" gap between the modern and the other sectors should be narrowed. Thus, data for all of the measures mentioned above would need to be collected by states or regions within a country. A measure of progress, therefore, would be the growth of the backward areas in relation to the more advanced.

Our profile, then, would consist of five indices in addition to GNP. They leave much to be desired and would even if the attendant task of data collection did not lie beyond the capability of most developing countries at present. Quantitative yardsticks by themselves cannot measure every dimension of progress. Statistics are not always the same as facts, and some facts are ascertainable only through qualitative analysis.

ANALYTICAL TOOLS

The art of analysis of human resources problems is, unfortunately, quite undeveloped. Until the last few years, neither employment nor skill generation were considered as core problems in economic development planning. Economists, for the most part, simply assumed that these problems would be resolved if the growth of national income could be accelerated. Manpower and education specialists, as a rule, were given rather low status in the hierarchy of development-planning organizations. As a consequence, there are few tools of analysis of human resources problems, and most of these are rather unsophisticated. Thus, the advocate of the human resources approach cannot rely on existing methodology; he is forced to suggest new and mostly unproven systems of analysis. We shall make a cursory examination of the "state of the art" along with some suggestions for new ventures.

1. *Manpower inventories*

Most countries attempt to make some kind of inventory of manpower at least in the modern sectors. The employment status of individuals can be included in the periodic censuses. A more detailed and accurate method, the establishment survey, is made by questionnaire, interviews, or a combination of both for all employing institutions above a specified size (usually ten employees). A good example of the latter is the annual enumeration in Kenya which requires all medium- and large-scale employers (both public and private) to report each year on individual employees, giving occupation, pay, and information on some other pertinent conditions of employment. There are, however, three important shortcomings in most employment inventory programs. First, occupational categories are often poorly selected and inadequately defined; second, the time gap between collection and publication of data is sometimes very great (as long as five years), making much of the data obsolete; and finally, employment inventories characteristically concentrate on modern-sector wage and salary employment, usually ignoring the traditional as well as important parts of the intermediate sectors.

Although the technical problems of making manpower inventories and labor-force surveys are not insolvable, most developing countries simply lack the personnel and financial resources to undertake them.

Knowledge about the dimensions and operation of labor markets is thus largely impressionistic, except perhaps for employment in the modern sectors which involve only a tiny proportion of the labor force as a whole. Thus, further research in this area is urgently needed in the developing countries, and it will be of critical importance for implementation of any kind of human resources approach to development planning.

2. *The manpower requirements approach to education planning*

During the sixties the major thrust of manpower analysis has been directed to determination of future requirements for formal education, particularly at the secondary and higher levels. In essence, the manpower requirements approach to education planning is an attempt to estimate needed educational outputs from a set of projections of economic growth forecasts or targets. These are used to determine output and employment in the various sectors of the economy. From the distribution of employment sector, an occupational distribution is then specified. Assumptions are then made concerning appropriate levels of formal education for each occupation. Estimates of the required number of persons by education level are then used in conjunction with data on existing employment, expected retirements and replacements, and new net requirements to meet expected expansion. The manpower requirement approach has been used rather extensively in Nigeria, Zambia, Tanzania, Kenya, and in the so-called Mediterranean Regional Project Countries (Turkey, Spain, Yugoslavia, Greece, and Portugal). A summary of my analysis of this approach in a previous work follows.[2]

There is no generally accepted methodology for estimating future requirements. Nor is there a clear concept of the meaning of the term "future requirements." Some people talk about "predicting" or "forecasting" manpower requirements; others contend that they are making "projections." And still others, emphasize the process of forward "target-setting."

---

2. Frederick H. Harbison and Charles A. Myers, *op. cit.,* Chap. 9.

A rather simple method of estimating future requirements is to ask existing establishments to specify them. This will provide an informed judgment of short-term requirements, but it is quite unreliable for long-run estimates. The establishments which may be in existence ten or twenty years hence may not be at all the same as the present ones. Furthermore, most employers are unwilling or unable to estimate what employment will be in the long run. As one exasperated owner of a business in Jordan is reported as saying, "Such guessing is an impious act, for only Allah knows what the future may hold." For these reasons, we consider that forecasts made by individual establishments are essentially part of an assessment of the present situation rather than a practical means of making long-run estimates.

Another method is to use past trends as a means of projecting future requirements.[3] This method has been used in some advanced countries to estimate needs for high-level scientific and engineering manpower as well as for teachers. The procedure is to extrapolate past trends in the growth of the number of persons in the particular occupation and then correlate this with total employment, production, population, gross national product, or some combination of such variables. The regression table thus obtained is then used to project future requirements for each occupation. This projection method has the advantage of simplicity, but its usefulness is limited. In many countries it is impossible to get past data for an adequate time series. And even where the data may be available, the assumption that future relationships can be derived from past trends is open to question.

A more complicated method is based upon the estimation of changes in productivity as the critical factor. The steps in this approach are the following.[4]

3. See *Forecasting Manpower Needs for the Age of Science* (Paris: OEEC, 1960); S. O. Doos, "Forecasting Manpower Requirements by Occupational Categories," prepared for Training Course for Human Resource Strategists, Frascati, Italy, September 1962 (Paris: OECD) (mimeographed); and National Science Foundation, *The Long Range Demand for Scientific and Technical Personnel, a Methodological Study* (Washington, D.C., 1961).
4. Herbert S. Parnes, *Forecasting Educational Needs for Economic and So-*

1. A manpower inventory is made along the lines which were described earlier.

2. The patterns of output for the various sectors of the economy are projected for the forecast year, usually as set forth in an economic-development plan. Then total employment for the economy as well as for each sector is estimated on the basis of some assumptions about productivity.

3. For each sector, the total employment for the forecast year is allocated among the various occupations according to the occupational classification system which has been chosen. Then the requirements for each occupational category are aggregated from the various sectors to give the total stocks required in the forecast year. Here, however, allowance must be made for the effects of increases in productivity on the occupational structure. As productivity increases, of course, the proportion of persons in high-level occupations increases relatively to those in the lesser skilled jobs. In practice, however, one must have assumptions regarding the influence of productivity increases on occupational structure since there are very little reliable data on which to base objective calculations.

4. The supply of personnel with each major type of educational qualification is estimated for the forecast year on the basis of present stocks, anticipated outflows from the existing educational system as presently planned, and allowances for losses due to death, retirement, and other reasons for withdrawal from the labor force.

5. The estimated outputs from the educational system are compared with the required outputs as determined in step 4.

6. The orders of magnitude for expansion of the educational system are then established to close the gap between anticipated requirements and presently expected supply.

This method, perhaps, has the greatest appeal to economic-development planners, and with modifications it has been used by most

---

cial Development, Mediterranean Regional Project (Paris: OECD, October 1962), and also Wilfred Beckerman, "Methodology for Projection of Educational Requirements," *Mediterranean Regional Project* (Paris: OECD, 1962) (mimeographed).

of the countries in the Mediterranean Regional Project. It links manpower requirements to productivity; it is designed to identify high-level manpower bottlenecks which could hamper production; and thus it appears logically to relate human resources needs to economic requirements.

This approach, however, has some shortcomings. First, although the productivity criterion may be appropriate for the manufacturing, construction, mining, and transportation sectors, it is not so useful for estimating high-level manpower requirements in public health, general activities of governments, and many kinds of services.

Second, a very troublesome problem is the lack of empirical data on which to base estimates of expected increases in productivity and the bearing of these on changes in occupational requirements. In practice, one can do little more here than to make general assumptions. For example, one may assume that in the forecast year the average productivity of all factories in a particular sector will equal the present productivity of the most modern ones. Or can one assume that average productivity of the manufacturing sector in Country A in the forecast year will approximate present productivity of a comparable sector in Country B, which is somewhat more advanced.[5]

A third problem which is inherent in this approach as well as in most others is the arbitrary determination (on the basis of assumptions) of educational requirements of high-level manpower for the forecast year. In very few cases are there precise or binding relationships between jobs and educational attainment. Indeed, in any occupational category, there may be a wide possible range of substitution among persons with various levels and kinds of education and train-

5. For example, a Puerto Rican manpower survey made in 1957 assumed that industrial productivity in that country would rise by 1975 to the level of the United States in 1950, and that parallel occupational groups should have equivalent educational requirements. The survey of manpower and education requirements in Italy made its productivity calculation (except for agriculture) by assuming that in 1975 productivity would reach that attained by France in 1960. For further discussion of problems of productivity assumptions see Parnes, *op. cit.,* and Michel Debeauvais, "Methods of Forecasting Long-term Manpower Needs," paper prepared for Training Course for Human Resource Strategists, Paris: OECD.

ing. In many cases, moreover, the demand for persons with particular levels of education may be dependent upon the available supply.

A final major shortcoming is that wages and salaries are not specified. Clearly, no realistic assessment of supply and demand for persons in critical occupations can be made without consideration of relative levels of compensation. Thus, the manpower requirements approach really projects only "needs" or targets for what is thought to be a desirable output of educational institutions. This is quite different from "effective demand," or actual expected employment of persons at stated wage and salary levels.

The "track record" of the manpower requirements approach has not been impressive. In most cases countries have become submerged in data collection and analysis problems, and as a result many manpower assessments are out of date before they are finished. Powerful ministries are likely to ignore or even block publication of reports which appear to be at odds with established policy. The personnel engaged in manpower assessments are often looked upon as "statistics chasers" rather than policy planners. For the most part, therefore, estimations of manpower requirements have had little practical impact on education planning except in a few countries. The manpower assessments in Tanzania, however, are a notable exception. Though not technically as sophisticated as recent surveys in some other countries, they have been more current, and above all they have been used as the basis for education planning as well as allocating bursaries for students entering higher education. If the dual criteria of practical design and operational usefulness are accepted, the Tanzania surveys are without question the best that have been developed in the African countries if not in the entire Third World.

3. The Tinbergen-Correa Model

Another widely employed technique for making rough estimates of required aggregate expansion in secondary and higher education is the Tinbergen-Correa approach.[6] It has been used in India as well

6. Hector Correa and Jan Tinbergen, "Quantitative Adaptation of Education to Accelerated Growth," *Kyklos,* Vol. 15 (1962), pp. 776-85.

as in some African countries. It is a simpler approach than the man-power requirements method and requires much less data. Using what they call a simple model of the input-output type, the authors attempt to relate directly needed secondary and higher educational outputs to given rates of economic growth, without using the intermediate step of calculating occupational requirements. Essentially, the number of persons required from each educational level is calculated from a series of linear equations which relate the stock of persons completing a given level of education and the number of students in each level to the aggregated volume of production. Its purpose is to suggest what structure of the educational system is needed in order to "let the economy grow at a certain rate" and how that structure should change with changes in the growth rate.

Certainly, the mathematical formulation of this model offers no grounds for criticism, but the assumptions implicit in the use of certain technical coefficients are open to question. For example, it is assumed that the number of persons with secondary education and also with higher education is proportional to the volume of production in the same time period. Such an assumption is based upon judgment pure and simple. Likewise, the coefficients expressing teacher-student ratios are based upon rather questionable assumptions, those actually used being derived from United States experience. Depending upon one's judgment, of course, coefficients derived from other countries could be used, or perhaps they might even be artificially constructed.

Another implied assumption in the Tinbergen-Correa model is that in the present situation the number of persons with secondary and higher education is the correct number for the existing level of aggregated production. In practice, however, there are usually acute shortages or even sizable surpluses. Moreover, this model implicitly assumes that technology and productivity in the time period remain constant, and it thus completely overlooks what effect such factors might have on required occupations and hence required educational qualifications. Finally, the model as presently developed draws no distinction between types of education (technical or academic), makes no allowance for qualitative imbalances in school curricula, and fails to distinguish between the major economic sectors of the economy.

In conclusion, the practical use of the Tinbergen-Correa model, as well as other approaches, depend upon the validity of the assumptions made with respect to empirical facts. To the extent that empirical evidence is unavailable, one must make judgments. Thus this model, although giving the appearance of methodological precision, is actually no less dependent upon guesswork than any other approach. To be sure, when empirical evidence becomes available, the assumptions regarding the technical coefficients may be changed accordingly. Likewise, the model can and should be expanded to include other variables, such as increases in productivity, and with refinements it could be used to make estimates for educated manpower by occupation and by sector.

4. *The rate of return approach*

The method which is most appealing to economists for allocating resources to human resources development is the rate of return approach based upon cost-benefit analysis. The idea that education is an important contributor to economic growth, of course, is not new. The concept of investment in human capital was included by Adam Smith in *The Wealth of Nations*. As early as 1925, a Russian economist, S. G. Strumilin estimated rates of return on various levels of education.[7] T. W. Schultz, Gary Becker, and others have developed the concept and tools of analysis for use in the United States. More recently, several economists have applied the rate of return approach to education planning in the developing countries.[8]

The rate of return approach is based upon the relationship between

7. S. G. Struminlin, "The Economic Significance of National Education," in *The Economics of Education,* edited by E. A. G. Robinson and J. E. Vaisey (London: International Economics Association, 1966), pp. 276-323.
8. A listing of some of the more important writings up to 1967 is given in Samuel Bowles, *Planning Educational Systems for Economic Growth* (Cambridge, Mass.: Harvard University Press, 1969), p. 153. Some other recent writings are *Lucila Arrigazzi,* "Evaluating the Expansion of a Vocational

two basic sets of data: (1) earnings data classified by levels and kinds of formal schooling as well as by age of members of the employed working force and (2) data on direct costs of schooling, together with estimates of indirect costs such as foregone earnings. In some cases information is taken from census data but more often from sample surveys. It could be readily available also from "tracer studies" described later in this chapter. As summarized by Maureen Woodhall in her case study of Colombia,[9] the basic calculation involves "a comparison of pre-tax earnings differentials and the total costs of education to society as a whole (including expenditures on teachers, books, etc., the value of buildings and the production foregone by society because of the decision to educate students instead of enrolling them in the labor market)" giving the "social rate of return to education," and "a comparison of post-tax earnings differentials and the costs of education borne by the individual (including fees, expenditures on books and earnings foregone)" giving "the private rate of return." The classic assumption made in dealing with this productive investment, hence the rationale for measuring the economic benefits of education to society by individual earnings differentials, is that the workers' earnings represent their marginal product, determined by the free interaction of supply and demand. The cost-benefit approach, then, employs such empirical data as age-education-earnings profiles and annual earnings differentials in estimating the returns to various levels of education.

The policy implications are to give priority within the formal system to investment in that kind of education which promises the high-

---

Training Programme: A Chilean Experience" (Paris: UNESCO, IIEP, March 20, 1969); *T. Paul Schultz,* "Returns to Education in Bogota, Colombia" (Santa Monica: The Rand Corporation, September 1968); *Marcelo Selowsky,* "The Effect of Unemployment as a Guide to Resource Allocation in Education: A Case Study on India" (Paris: UNESCO, IIEP, June 20, 1969); *Hans Heinrich Thias,* "Cost-Benefit Analysis in Education: A Case Study on Kenya" (Washington: IBRD, November 1969); *Maureen Woodhall,* "The Use of Cost-Benefit Analysis to Compare the Rates of Return at Different Education Levels: A Case Study in Colombia" (Paris: UNESCO, IIEP, March 7, 1969).
9. Maureen Woodhall, *op. cit.*

est returns and to make overall allocations to education on the basis of comparison of returns to investment in other sectors. This kind of analysis, obviously, assumes that maximization of aggregate income is the supreme target of development planning.

A much more sophisticated approach, based also on cost-benefit analysis, is Bowles's linear programming model for efficient allocation of resources in education.[10] It requires, first, a description of various combinations of mutually consistent, feasible enrollment levels, given the total supply of factors. It then evaluates the advisability of each of the constituent patterns of enrollment and use of resources. A standard of evaluation, called the "objective function," is constructed to select the most desirable enrollment pattern. Finally, the productivity of resources (in income generation) in the educational system is compared with the productivity of resources in other areas of the economy to determine the total available resources to be allocated to that system. The Bowles model is a powerful analytical tool, and its application to the educational systems of Greece and Northern Nigeria is quite enlightening.

There are many technical questions related to the methodology of the rate of return and linear programming approaches which need not be dwelt upon here. Few developing countries, moreover, have adequate statistics on earnings of persons with different levels of education nor on factors other than formal schooling, which may explain part of the earnings differentials. We shall turn our own attention to the more fundamental conceptual issues.

First, in most developing countries there is good reason to doubt that relative earnings of individuals reflect either their marginal or average productivity or their value to society. In many cases, earnings are determined more by institutional than by market forces, reflecting wage and salary structures based upon tradition, class, or previous colonial administrations. The calculation of social returns, for example, must be based upon more than income. Obviously a scientist who works in a research organization which is applying scientific knowledge to development problems would be valued more

10. Samuel Bowles, *op. cit.,* particularly Chap. IV.

highly than a university graduate who performs routine duties in a ministry, despite the fact that both may receive approximately the same salary. Or, although his salary may be substantially lower, the agricultural assistant who teaches hundreds of farmers the arts of seed selection and modern cultivation methods may be more valuable than the agronomist who shuffles papers in the ministry headquarters. And how would one evaluate the services of a physician whose practice is largely among high salaried expatriates in comparison with the services of the public health doctor who directly or indirectly ministers to the masses?

A second shortcoming, related to the first, is that the rate of return and linear programming approaches completely ignore the measurement of effectiveness of education as a selection device, as a means of building consensus, as a process of enrichment of human life, and as an instrument for development of *strategic* skills and knowledge. Income is certainly not an adequate proxy for any of these central functions of education. Economists may claim, with some justification, that the measurement of such intangibles is not their business; nevertheless, those charged with responsibility for broadly based national development must weigh them carefully.

Finally, even within the narrow boundaries of responsibility of the economist, the rate of return approach tends to bypass the critical issues of income and opportunity distribution. In looking at this as well as his own model, Bowles reluctantly concludes: "This shortcoming is important because we desire social justice as well as a large gross national product, and there is no reason to expect that the pattern of educational development which maximizes the rate of economic growth will at the same time generate an equitable distribution of income."[11]

The manpower requirements approach, the Tinbergen-Correa model, and the rate of return analysis do not provide, either individually or in combination, very reliable guidelines for investment in education. Bowles has made a penetrating analysis of their comparative usefulness, and he has also shown that, in practical application, each

11. *Ibid.*, pp. 207-8.

may have quite different policy implications.[12] As yet, none of these approaches has in fact had a great deal of influence on educational planning, except in the case of the manpower approach to planning in Tanzania mentioned above.

5. *The social objectives method*

Unlike the manpower and rate of return approaches which attempt to relate education to development needs and income generation, the "social objectives method" places great stress on noneconomic objectives of education. This method concentrates, therefore, on identifying deficiencies in the present educational system in the light of social and educational objectives, and it projects future needs in terms of estimated population increases and the desire of persons for education at various levels. Certain goals are taken for granted, such as elimination of illiteracy, increasing enrollment ratios in secondary education, decreasing the student-teacher ratios to desirable levels, lowering wastage rates, and improvement of standards. These goals, in effect, are suggested by making comparisons with other countries. Then the targets for future development are based upon a statistical calculation of the logistics and cost of satisfying these goals in varying periods of time.

This approach has been favored traditionally by educators. It bypasses completely the difficult determination of occupational requirements. But at the same time, it overlooks essential economic problems. If this approach is used, there is likely to be little integration of the work of the educational planners and the economic planners, and in the end the latter are likely to recommend that expenditures for education, along with other social activities, be given a lower priority that investments in projects which are clearly productive and appear to contribute more directly to economic growth.

6. *"Tracer studies" as measurement tools for effectiveness of the learning system*

The "tracer study" idea is suggested by the tracer bullet which lights its path from the firing point to the target. It is nothing more

12. *Ibid.,* Chap. VI.

nor less than a system for following the work experiences of those who leave or complete programs of education or training, either formal or informal. Admittedly, such follow-up studies are difficult and expensive, but the returns in terms of effective project evaluation and feedback to skill- and knowledge-generating institutions, are potentially very great.

The objective of most tracer studies has been to collect data on how secondary school or university graduates get jobs, how long they take to find work, their levels of compensation, relevance of previous education to work experience, and career pathways in general. They can provide information on the linkages between education and the world of work; they give in-depth data on unemployment or under-employment of educated manpower; and they are useful in supplying hard facts for vocational counseling. An initial pilot tracer study in Kenya illustrates some of the questions which may be raised about projects of this kind.

In 1969, the Institute for Development Studies at the University of Nairobi conducted a pilot tracer study of fourth-form secondary schools in Kenya. A small team of researchers at IDS worked in collaboration with the headmasters and careermasters in the selected schools. The basic tracing instrument was a simple card file for each leaver on which was recorded basic facts from school records about each student's family background and educational history. The post-school employment tracing process was first attempted by mail questionnaires. Students not located in this way were traced by a variety of procedures, including questioning of friends still in school, parents, and others who could supply information about their whereabouts, and eventually, project personnel were assigned to search out the missing leavers in person. Within a very short time, the research team was able to trace 93 per cent of the leavers from the sample schools. Once traced, the leavers were asked to supply information concerning their occupation, pay, method and time of finding employment, and other relevant questions. In some cases, employers were also asked for supplementary information.

Experience with the pilot study in Kenya indicates:

1. Most school leavers can be traced to their places of employment, but follow-up personal interviews are necessary to supplement mail questionnaires.
2. Information about work experience and conditions of employment can be secured easily, but analysis of the data collected involved more time and expense than originally estimated.
3. School headmasters and careermasters are eager to make use of the information received on employment experience and career pathways.
4. Estimates of unemployed school leavers derived from the tracer studies were at variance with estimates derived from a Kenya manpower survey (the employment rate being much lower in the case of the tracer studies).
5. Schools, and probably also universities, will require inducement, either in the form of grants or extra personnel, to undertake tracer studies.

The tracer study device probably could be generalized and systematized in most countries. A first step would be a requirement that every major institution conducting education or training programs establish a simple but standardized system for tracing their outputs for a period of from two to five years. Placing the responsibility for tracing on the education or training institution would constitute in itself an important means of building better linkages between the learning system and the system of employment generation; it would make the institutions more sensitive to employment and possibly lead to more realistic orientation of the curricula to the world of work; and it would enable them to carry out more effective counseling and guidance services for their students.

The tracer study idea, of course, is not new. Many researchers have made follow-up studies of students in education and training programs; indeed, that would be required in any serious exercise of project evaluation. But most follow-up studies are too elaborate, complicated, and expensive to be undertaken by already overworked headmasters or directors of training programs. The primary considerations for a generalized tracer system would be simplicity of administration, ease of collecting information, and capability of analysis by relatively unskilled persons without use of complicated data processing systems. The design of such a program, however, would require a great deal of experimentation and systematic research.

There may be other ways of establishing a generalized tracer system. For example, in Kenya a proposal is under consideration to combine the tracer idea with the annual labor force enumeration by employers. Under this scheme, each school or university leaver would be assigned a serial number coded to identify the school, courses of study, grades, and years of attendance. The leaver would keep this serial number for his working life, and his employer would be required to record it on all returns made on the annual enumeration. With this procedure the pre-employment school record of each employee with secondary education and above could be traced easily. Reports on post-school employment could be made to headmasters, careermasters, or university officials for all leavers. As information of this kind is accumulated each year, there would be a complete individual record of changes in occupation, pay, promotion, and transfer—in other words, a complete tracing of career pathways. The information collected could be used also by research organizations for making cost-effectiveness studies, identifying major shifts in employment patterns, estimating manpower supply and demand, and developing materials for guidance purposes. This scheme, moreover, might eliminate the necessity of making periodic manpower surveys by substituting a procedure which in effect would be a continuous process of assessment of the market for middle- and high-level manpower in relationship to the educational system. There are, however, some drawbacks and knotty questions. The scheme is more appropriate for tracing the history of employment than experience with unemployment. The assignment of serial numbers and securing the compliance of employers in reporting serial numbers might pose some problems, and the reporting itself could infringe upon individual civil liberties. The analysis of the data might also create obstacles in newly developing countries, particularly if the system were extended beyond secondary and higher education to all primary schools and other learning institutions. Nevertheless, the possibilities for building more effective linkages between school and work are so great that they warrant serious consideration in most countries.

In conclusion, the most useful function of tracer studies is analysis of relationships between learning institutions and the world of work. If used widely, they could chart trends and provide warning signals indicating areas of imbalance between the learning and employment generation systems. They could supply much of the information required to determine the benefits of education and training programs. They have, of course, obvious limitations. In common with most other analytical tools, they are more easily applied to manpower in the modern than in the intermediate and traditional sectors. They record past actions, and by themselves provide no forward estimates. Finally, the costs could be high and the implementation cumbersome. Clearly, the design of a nationwide tracer system is a formidable task and would require extensive experimentation.

7. *The rural learning service survey*

As mentioned above, the traditional manpower survey is a limited-purpose instrument designed primarily to estimate the need for secondary school and university graduates in modern-sector employment. It would still be useful in the human resources approach. The larger and more difficult task, however, would be the assessment of learning needs in relationship to employment opportunities for the less educated members of the labor force and in particular for those living in rural areas. For example, the terms of reference for a rural learning service survey in a district or region might include the following.

1. Assessment of current employment status of the population living in the district or region, covering those engaged in subsistence farming, cash-crop agriculture, industries, commerce, and public services.

2. Setting of opportunity targets on the basis of a local development plan aimed at maximum feasible employment generation and improvement in levels of living of persons in subsistence agriculture.

3. Assessment of all existing learning programs specifying numbers of participants, orientation of education and training provided, facilities, program, staff, and operation. Where possible this would include cost-effectiveness analysis of the principal activities and appraisal of major thrusts of needed expansion in the learning system.

4. Specification of learning objectives in relation to expected employment opportunities and determination of responsibility for sponsorship and administration of the various formal and nonformal education and training programs involved.

5. Determination of requirements for extended or new learning services geared to expected employment opportunities, including cost of construction of facilities and plans for selection and training of staff.

6. Preparation of a local learning service budget, including some mechanism of grants-in-aid from the central government to maintain the mixture of learning services deemed to be most essential.

7. Design of a mechanism for monitoring the various programs in the local learning system, using tracer studies as a basis for continuous review of the gearing of learning services to work opportunities.

Obviously, such an ambitious effort would depend upon the planning function being decentralized, as well as on the availability of competent personnel to carry it forward at the local level. Within the next decade, however, many countries may undertake such tasks on a pilot basis in a number of rural areas, and this in itself would be a significant forward step.

8. *Conclusion on the relevance of analytical tools*

By any standard, the availability of analytical tools for planning the development and utilization of human resources leaves much to be desired. Most have been used only for analysis of modern-sector requirements and thus are relevant to only a small proportion of the labor force. Both the manpower requirements and rate of return approaches are captives of a framework which assumes that maximization of national income is the supreme goal of developing societies.

The social objective approach is little more than a rationalization for providing more of the same kind of education, despite the obvious lack of effective gearing between education and employment. The tracer study idea is new and as yet not operational in the developing countries. The rural learning-needs survey is nothing more than a prospectus for looking at human resources problems at the grass roots level and is not in itself an analytical tool.

There is, however, no cause for despair. Many of the analytical tools described above, with relatively minor changes, · could be adapted to the human resource approach. The Bowles-type linear programming model could be adapted to estimating employment and skill generation as the principal target rather than income maximization. Manpower assessments can be extended to skills and knowledge needs outside of the modern sector. Evaluations of effectiveness of learning programs need not be confined to formal schooling but can be extended to farmer-training centers, skill development during employment, and other strategic nonformal education programs. There is no controversy over existing concepts of calculating costs of both formal and nonformal education and training programs. The central problem is the measurement of effectiveness, not just with respect to income but in terms of other objectives as well.

THE STRATEGY OF PLANNING

For years, special pleaders have argued that manpower and education problems are central rather than peripheral to the processes of growth. Manpower planning and education planning, they contend, should be integral components of national development planning. In many countries there are now manpower or human resources sections in national planning organizations, but this does not by any means imply the adoption of the human resources approach. Quite the reverse. Their function is mainly to collect statistics on the supply and demand for labor and perhaps to make high-level manpower surveys geared to planning goals set from the GNP perspective. But seldom do they have much influence in establishing the goals themselves. By contrast, in the human resources approach all divisions of the planning organization would be guided by human resources considerations as the point of departure for target-setting and program determination. Thus a specialized human resources division would be an anachronism. From top to bottom the main concern of all planners would be to design a development strategy to maximize employment and learning opportunities.

The human resources approach would shift research priorities and the perspective of project evaluation. For example, the employment implications of investment in various industries and services would be estimated with great care; the skill-generating potential of foreign-owned enterprises would be examined more closely; rural development would become less centered on increasing aggregate yields on large farms and more concerned with the dissemination of new technologies to the largest possible number of producers; and much of the scientific and engineering research effort would be directed toward invention of modern capital-stretching technologies. As suggested in Chapter 2, industrialization would become more outward-looking in promoting labor-intensive manufactures for export. Economists would give more attention to the implications of wage and salary increases for new employment generation; and minimum wage and labor legislation would be subject to more critical review. Finally, taxation, exchange rates, and subsidies would have to be altered in order to provide greater incentives for employment generation.

In short, although the planning process would still be dominated by economists, they might build different models and use their econometric tools to look at more than national income generation. Their techniques might be the same, but the "game plan" would be different.

8 | In Conclusion

Nation-building can be viewed from many perspectives. To some it means progress in creating a credible and viable political system. Others view it as a process of social modernization. For many leaders of the new nations, it is the achievement of independence of sovereign status. To most economists and planners, development is growth in national income or GNP. This volume presents another point of view: human resources as the wealth of nations.

In the human resources approach the goals of development are the maximum possible utilization of human beings in more productive activity and the fullest possible development of the skills, knowledge, and capacities of the labor force which are pertinent to such activity. Productive activity is broadly defined to include not only production of material goods and services but also the work of artists, musicians, writers, philosophers, theologians, statesmen, and all others participating in the modernization process. In this definition they are all members of the labor force. The underlying premise of this approach is that a nation which is unable to develop and utilize its labor force effectively will be unable to develop anything else. Accordingly, the strategy of development centers on human rather than material agents.

In this perspective, the developing countries are confronted with two major problems: first, pervasive underutilization of the capacities of human beings as manifested by rising unemployment and

157

underemployment in both rural and urban areas, brought about in part by high rates of population growth; and second, the underdevelopment of the capacities of human agents for productive use of their energies. The solutions are to be found in economywide employment generation and the building of nationwide learning systems encompassing all formal as well as nonformal education. In the human resources perspective, the formulation of development strategies would begin with consideration of these problems.

The problems of human resources utilization and development were explored in some detail in Chapters 2-5. The human resources approach as such was outlined in Chapter 6, while some of the methodological difficulties in its implementation were mentioned in Chapter 7. Its major themes can be briefly summarized.

First, there is no serious conflict between maximizing employment opportunities and maximizing national income. The more productive employment of a country's vast reservoir of underutilized human resources will increase its national income. The case was made in Chapters 2 and 6 that a rise in GNP is the likely consequence of more effective utilization and development of human resources. Here the differences between the human resources and the GNP approaches are minor. Indeed, in the human resources approach, employment opportunity for the masses of the population outside of modern-sector labor markets must be measured by their real incomes. To be sure, the GNP approach emphasizes aggregate income growth, but it pays less attention to distribution. The human resources approach, by emphasizing the generation of better employment opportunities for *all* segments in the labor force, stresses distribution more directly and gives it higher priority. It is centrally concerned with *who shares* in productive activity as well as with *what* and *how much* is produced. It would give priority to removing disparities between the rich and the poor and between the highly educated and the less educated, as well as to increasing aggregate wealth expressed either in terms of material things or human capability.

Second, the fullest possible development of the skills, knowledge, and capacities of the labor force involves a broad learning process. Formal schooling is a fundamental part of this process, but working environments themselves and a wide range of nonformal training activities play strategic roles as well. In today's developing countries, the human resources approach would stress universal learning opportunities for adults and children alike. It would seek to build formal education and other relevant learning activities into a comprehensive and cohesive nationwide learning system geared closely to present and future opportunities for productive work. According to this logic, universal learning opportunity is a goal of higher priority than universal primary education for children of school age, although both are important for effective nation-building. A cardinal principle is that great emphasis must be placed on lifelong, recurrent learning.

Finally, one can be both pessimistic and optimistic about the future development of the Third World countries. The generation of more productive employment opportunities for all is probably beyond the reach of most countries which continue to have high rates of population growth. A country struggling to improve its levels of living when population is increasing at 2½ or 3 per cent a year may be likened to a man weighing 250 or 300 pounds trying to compete in a marathon run; both have too much to drag. But, one can be much more optimistic about developing the skills and knowledge of man, for his capacity for learning is virtually limitless. Thus, by striving to build effective nationwide learning systems, all countries may prosper even if they are poorly endowed with material wealth or natural resources.

It is quite unlikely, of course, that any country will ever adopt the human resources approach completely in planning its development strategy. Indeed, few have ever followed logically and consistently the GNP approach. In practice, development strategies are the outgrowth of an amalgamation of different perspectives and compromises on conflicting goals. In suggesting a logic for development, the social scientist should never hope to usurp the prerogatives of the decision makers.

In recent years, many persons, including labor economists, both within and outside the Third World countries, have complained about the neglect of the "human factor" in the conceptualization of economic growth. But, paradoxically, nearly everyone agrees that human beings after all are the only actors on the stage of development. Instead of joining the chorus of those who criticize the more orthodox approach of economists and who call for the "dethronement of GNP," an attempt has been made in this volume to present an overall, systematic logic for national development from the point of view of a human resources economist.

Selected Bibliography

The body of written materials on education, training, and employment in developing countries is already large, and it is growing rapidly. The selected sources which follow are particularly useful for more extensive understanding of the problems of development and utilization of human resources. The listings were compiled in May 1972. Important new sources are constantly being added because of the rapid expansion of interest and writing in this field.

General

Education and World Affairs, Committee on Education and Human Resource Development, *Nigerian Human Resource Development and Utilization,* New York: 1967.

————, Committee on the International Migration of Talent, *The International Migration of High Level Manpower,* New York: Praeger Publishers, 1970.

————, ————, *Modernization and the Migration of Talent,* New York: 1970.

Ginzberg, Eli, *Manpower for Development,* New York: Praeger Publishers, 1971.

————, *Perspectives on Indian Manpower, Employment and Income,* New York: Columbia University, Conservation of Human Resources, 1971.

Harbison, Frederick H., Joan Maruhnic and Jane R. Resnick, *Quantitative Analyses of Modernization and Development,* Princeton, N.J.: Princeton University, Industrial Relations Section, 1970.

Heyer, Judith et al., *Rural Development in Kenya: A Survey of Fourteen Districts with Recommendations for Intensified Development,* Nairobi: University College, Institute for Development Studies, 1969.

Marsden, Keith, "Towards a Synthesis of Economic Growth and Social Justice," *International Labour Review,* Vol. 100, No. 5 (Nov. 1969), pp. 389-418.

Shaw, Robert d'A., *Rethinking Economic Development* (Headline Series No. 208), New York: Foreign Policy Association, 1971.

Tanzania, *Second Five-Year Plan for Economic and Social Development* (4 vols.), Dar es Salaam: Government Printer, 1969.

Thomas, Robert L., *The Work of the Manpower Planning Unit in Africa,* Dakar: African Institute for Economic Development, 1969.

Tobias, George, *Human Resources in India,* New Delhi: Meenakshi Prakashan, 1971.

U. S. Department of Labor, Bureau of Labor Statistics, *How to Make an Inventory of High-Level and Skilled Manpower in Developing Countries* (BLS Report No. 331), Washington, D.C.: 1968.

————, ————, *Summaries of Manpower Surveys and Reports for Developing Countries, 1958-1968* (Bulletin No. 1628), Washington, D.C.: Government Printing Office, 1969.

Zambia, Development Division, *Zambian Manpower,* Lusaka: Government Printer, 1969.

Formal and Nonformal Education

Adams, Don K. and Robert M. Bjord, *Education in Developing Areas,* New York: David McKay Co., 1969.

Alexander-Frutschi, Marian (ed.), *Issues in Occupational Education and Training,* New Delhi: Orient Longmans, 1970.

Anderson, C. Arnold and Mary Jean Bowman (eds.), *Education and Economic Development,* Chicago: Aldine Publishing Co., 1965.

Ashby, Eric, *Universities: British, Indian, African. A Study in the Ecology of Higher Education,* Cambridge: Harvard University Press, 1966.

Beeby, Clarence E., *The Quality of Education in Developing Countries,* Cambridge: Harvard University Press, 1966.

Bereday, George Z. F. (ed.), *Essays on World Education: The Crisis of Supply and Demand,* New York: Oxford University Press, 1969.

Blaug, Mark, *Economics of Education: A Selected Annotated Bibliography* (2nd ed.), New York: Pergamon Press, 1970.

————, *An Introduction to the Economics of Education,* London: Allen Lane The Penguin Press, 1970.

Callaway, Archibald, "Nigeria's Indigenous Education: The Apprenticeship System," *ODU,* A Journal of West African Studies (July 1964), pp. 67-79.

————, "School Leavers and Their Village Setting," *ODU* (April 1969), pp. 46-70.

Cameron, John, *The Development of Education in East Africa,* New York: Teachers College Press, 1970.

Coombs, Philip H., *The World Educational Crisis: A Systems Analysis,* New York: Oxford University Press, 1968.

———— and Jacques Hallak, *Managing Educationl Costs,* New York: Oxford University Press, 1972.

Davis, Russell C., *Planning Human Resource Development: Educational Models and Schemata,* Chicago: Rand McNally & Co., 1966.

Hunter, Guy, *Education for a Developing Region: A Study in East Africa,* London: George Allen and Unwin, 1963.

Harbison, Frederick H. and Charles A. Myers, *Education, Manpower and Economic Growth: Strategies of Human Resource Development,* New York: McGraw-Hill Book Co., 1964.

International Institute for Educational Planning, Fundamentals of Educational Planning Series:—

> No. 1. *What Is Educational Planning?* by Philip H. Coombs, Paris: 1970.
>
> No. 2. *The Relation of Educational Plans to Economic and Social Planning* by Raymond Poignant, Paris: 1969.
>
> No. 3. *Educational Planning and Human Resource Development* by Frederick H. Harbison, Paris: 1969.
>
> No. 4. *Planning and the Educational Administrator* by Clarence E. Beeby, Paris: 1969.
>
> No. 5. *The Social Context of Educational Planning* by C. Arnold Anderson, Paris: 1967.
>
> No. 6. *The Costing of Educational Plans* by John E. Vaizey and J. D. Chesswas, Paris: 1969.
>
> No. 7. *The Problems of Rural Education* by Vincent L. Griffiths, Paris: 1968.
>
> No. 8. *Educational Planning: The Adviser's Role* by Adam Curle, Paris: 1968.
>
> No. 9. *Demographic Aspects of Educational Planning* by Ta Ngoc Chau, Paris: 1969.
>
> No. 10. *The Analysis of Educational Costs and Expenditure* by Jacques Hallak, Paris: 1969.

No. 11. *The Professional Identity of the Educational Planner* by Adam Curle, Paris: 1969.

No. 12. *The Conditions for Success in Educational Planning* by G. C. Ruscoe, Paris: 1969.

No. 13. *Cost-Benefit Analysis in Educational Planning* by Maureen Woodhall, Paris: 1970.

International Institute for Educational Planning, *Manpower Aspects of Educational Planning: Problems for the Future,* Paris: 1968.

Machlup, Fritz, *Educational and Economic Growth,* Lincoln: University of Nebraska Press, 1970.

Nigeria, Federal Ministry of Education, *Investment in Education, The Report of the Commission on Post-School Certificate and Higher Education in Nigeria* (Eric Ashby, Chairman), Lagos: Federal Government Printer, 1960.

Robinson, Edward A. G. and John E. Vaizey (eds.), *The Economics of Education,* New York: St. Martin's Press, 1966.

Schultz, Theodore W., *Economic Value of Education,* New York: Columbia University Press, 1962.

————, *Investment in Human Capital: The Role of Education and of Research,* New York: Free Press, 1971.

Selowsky, Marcelo, *The Effect of Unemployment and Growth on the Rate of Return to Education: The Case of Colombia* (Economic Development Report 116), Cambridge: Harvard University, Center for International Affairs, 1968.

Sheffield, James R. and Victor P. Diejomaoh, *Non-Formal Education in African Development,* New York: African-American Institute, 1972.

Staley, Eugene, *Planning Occupational Education and Training for Development,* New Delhi: Orient Longmans, 1970.

United Nations Educational, Science and Cultural Organization, *An Asian Model of Educational Development: Perspectives for 1965-80,* Paris: 1966.

Employment Generation

Baer, Werner and Michael A. E. Herve, "Employment and Industrialization in Developing Countries," *Quarterly Journal of Economics,* Vol. 80, No. 1 (Feb. 1966), pp. 88-107.

Berg, Eliot J., *Wages and Employment in Less-Developed Countries* (Discussion Paper No. 13), Ann Arbor, Mich.: University of Michigan, Center for Research on Economic Development, 1970.

Blaug, Mark *et al., The Causes of Graduate Unemployment in India,* London: Allen Lane The Penguin Press, 1969.

Brown, Lester R., *The Seeds of Change: The Green Revolution and Development in the 1970's,* New York: Praeger Publishers, 1970.

Cambridge Conference on Development Problems, 7th, 1970, *Prospects for Employment Opportunities in the Nineteen Seventies,* Ronald Robinson and Peter Johnston (eds.), London: H. M. Stationery Office, 1971.

Conference on Manpower Problems in East and Southeast Asia (papers), Singapore: University of Singapore, May 1971.

Eicher, Carl *et al., Employment Generation in African Agriculture,* East Lansing, Mich.: Michigan State University, College of Agriculture and Natural Resources, Institute of International Agriculture, 1970.

Fei, John C. H. and Gustav Ranis, *Development of the Labor Surplus Economy: Theory and Policy,* Homewood, Ill.: Richard D. Irwin, 1964.

Frank, Charles R., Jr., *The Problem of Urban Unemployment in Africa* (Discussion Paper No. 16), Princeton, N.J.: Princeton University, Woodrow Wilson School of Public and International Affairs, Research Program in Economic Development, 1970.

Ghai, Dharam P., "Employment Performance, Prospects and Policies in Kenya," *East Africa Journal,* Vol. VII, No. X (Nov. 1970), pp. 4-11.

Harris, John R. and Michael P. Todaro, "Migration, Unemployment and Development: A Two-Sector Analysis," *American Economic Review,* Vol. LX, No. 1 (March 1970), pp. 126-42.

International Labour Office, *Essays on Employment* (selected and introduced by Walter Galenson), Geneva: 1971.

————, *Matching Employment Opportunities and Expectations: A Programme of Action for Ceylon* (2 vols.), Geneva: 1971.

————, *Towards Full Employment: A Programme for Colombia,* Geneva: 1970.

————, *The World Employment Programme,* Geneva: 1969.

International Labour Organization Third African Regional Conference, Accra, December 1969, *Employment Policy in Africa* (Report IV (2)), Geneva: International Labour Office, 1969.

Johnson, Glenn L. *et al., Strategies and Recommendations for Nigerian Rural Development, 1969/1985,* East Lansing, Mich.: Michigan State University, Consortium for the Study of Nigerian Rural Development, 1969.

Kerr, Clark *et al., Industrialism and Industrial Man* (2nd ed.), New York: Oxford University Press, 1964.

Kilby, Peter, *Industrialization in an Open Economy: Nigeria, 1945-1966,* Cambridge: Cambridge University Press, 1969.

Lewis, William Arthur, *Development Planning: The Essentials of Economic Policy,* New York: Harper & Row, 1966.

McNamara, Robert S., *Address to the Board of Governors,* Washington, D.C.: International Bank for Reconstruction and Development, 1971.

Myrdal, Gunnar, *Asian Drama: An Inquiry into the Poverty of Nations,* New York: Twentieth Century Fund, 1968.

Organization for Economic Cooperation and Development, *The Challenge of Unemployment to Development and the Role of Training and Research Institutes in Development,* Paris: 1971.

Oshima, Harry T., "Labor Force Explosion and the Labor Intensive Sector in Asian Growth," *Economic Development and Cultural Change,* Vol. 19, No. 2 (Jan. 1971), pp. 161-83.

Ridker, Ronald G., *Employment in South Asia: Problems, Prospects and Prescriptions* (Occasional Paper Series No. 1), Washington, D.C.: Overseas Development Council, 1971.

————— and Harold Lubell (eds.), *Employment and Unemployment Problems of the Near East and South Asia* (2 vols.), New Delhi: Vikas Publications, 1971.

Shaw, Robert d'A., *Jobs and Agricultural Development,* Washington, D.C.: Overseas Development Council, 1970.

Sheffield, James R. (ed.), *Education, Employment and Rural Development: The Proceedings of a Conference Held at Kericho, Kenya in September 1966,* Nairobi: East African Publishing House, 1967.

Staley, Eugene and Richard Morse, *Modern Small Industry for Developing Countries,* New York: McGraw-Hill Book Co., 1965.

Stewart, Frances and Paul Streeter, "Conflicts between Output and Employment Objectives in Developing Countries," *Oxford Economic Papers,* Vol. 23, No. 2 (July 1971), pp. 145-68.

Thorbecke, E. and E. Stoutjesdijk, *Employment and Output—A Methodology Applied to Peru and Guatemala,* Paris: Organization for Economic Cooperation and Development, 1971.

Todaro, Michael P., "A Model of Labor Migration and Urban Unemployment in Less Developed Countries," *American Economic Review,* Vol. LIX, No. 1 (March 1969), pp. 138-48.

Turnham, David, *The Employment Problem in Less Developed Countries: A Review of Evidence,* Paris: Organization for Economic Cooperation and Development, 1970.

Yudelman, Montague, *Technological Change in Agriculture and Employment in Developing Countries,* Paris: Organization for Economic Cooperation and Development, 1971.

Index